Fee-Based Services: Issues & Answers

Second Conference on Fee-Based Research in College and University Libraries

Proceedings of the meetings held at The University of Michigan
Ann Arbor, Michigan, May 10–12, 1987

Compiled by Anne K. Beaubien

Sponsored by Michigan Information Transfer Source (MITS)
The University of Michigan Libraries, Ann Arbor

Library of Congress Cataloging-in-Publication Data

Conference on Fee Based Research in College and
    University Libraries (2nd : 1987 : University of
    Michigan)
    Fee-based services: issues and answers

    Bibliography: pp 74–80
    Includes index.
    1. Library fines and fees—United States—Congresses.
2. Libraries, University and college—United States—
Finance—Congresses.   3. Information services—United
States—Fees—Congresses.   I. Beaubien, Anne K.
II. Michigan Information Transfer Source.   III. Title.
Z683.2.U6C66   1987   025.5'23'0973   87-34900

ISBN 0-9619861-0-7

Contents

Preface

Anne K. Beaubien
Head, Cooperative Access Services
University of Michigan Libraries
Ann Arbor, Michigan

The first conference on Fee Based Research in College and University Libraries was held in June, 1982 at the C. W. Post Center of Long Island University and sponsored by the Center for Business Research and the B. Davis Schwartz Memorial Library. It was organized by Mary McNierney Grant, Director of the Center for Business Research. Proceedings of that conference were published in 1983 by the C. W. Post Center.

John Beecher, formerly of the University of Minnesota, was one of the leaders who realized it was time to hold a second conference on fee-based services in academic libraries. He began organizing a conference for fall 1986 in Minneapolis, but he accepted the directorship at North Dakota State University and could not proceed with the idea. When I arrived at the American Library Association annual conference in New York in June 1986, I learned of John's aborted conference, and several members of FISCAL (ACRL Fee-Based Service Centers in Academic Libraries Discussion Group) urged me to consider hosting such a conference. The members felt strongly that the time was right and suggested I organize a conference for the spring of 1987. They argued that the midwest would be a good location, that Ann Arbor is a lovely place to visit, and that most people can easily get flights to Detroit.

I put together a proposed budget and program emphasizing speakers who have been involved with fee-based information services for a long time. This received enthusiastic support from Dr. Richard M. Dougherty, Director of Libraries, and Carla Stoffle, Deputy Director of Libraries at The University of Michigan. All of my first choice speakers accepted my invitation, and we began preparing the marketing for the conference. In total, fifty-seven participants from twenty-two states and Canada participated in the conference. They had many opportunities to talk with each other as well as listen to excellent speakers. The conference received rave evaluations from the attendees.

This conference brought to light just how much has happened in the intervening five years since the last one. There has been an increased awareness of the possibility of academic libraries providing library services for a fee to nonprimary clientele. Specific services vary but can include the provision of database searching, indepth research, document delivery, current awareness, indexing, translations, analysis of data, and the like. MITS (Michigan Information Transfer Source) was established in 1980, one of the first in the new wave of such services started in an academic library since the mid 1960s. Since 1985, MITS has been part of Cooperative Access Services, formed in that year, which reports to Carla Stoffle, Deputy Director of Libraries. Cooperative Access Services includes MITS, Interlibrary Loan (both borrowing and lending), a faculty microcomputer lab, and 747-FAST, a campus delivery service for faculty.

Professional library associations have responded to the development of fee-based services. The American Library Association, Association of College and Research Libraries (ACRL), established a discussion group on Fee-Based Information Service Centers in Academic (and Research) Libraries (FISCAL) in June 1982. It was co-founded by Elizabeth Lunden and Jim Thompson who, at that time, were both working for Rice University. At midwinter and annual ALA conferences, approximately sixty librarians attend FISCAL and discuss topics of common concern. AT the first FISCAL meeting in January of 1983, approximately five people in the room actually had a fee-based service and the rest were thinking about it. In 1987 about half the sixty people attending FISCAL had some type of fee-based service. FISCAL has been chaired by Liz Lunden, Berry Richards, Mary Grant, Anne Beaubien, and Kathy Tomajko will lead FISCAL in 1987-88. The Reference and Adult Services Division (RASD) of ALA has a committee on Fee-Based Reference Service, established in January, 1984. The Consultants Section of the Library Management Division of the Special Libraries Association was created in 1981 and has in its membership private consultants and information brokers.

Continuing education courses are offered by both ALA and Special Libraries Association. ALA's ACRL has had a continuing education course called "Considerations for Establishing & Marketing Fee-Based Services in Academic Libraries" since 1983–84 and SLA has a course, "Making Money: Fees for Information Service," which was selected as the 1986–87 Regional Program because increasing numbers of institutions are considering the use of fee-for-information utilities.[1] Private brokers are served by the Independent Librarians Roundtable in ALA as well as the Consultants Section in SLA. As a further indication of activity, the Philadelphia area information brokers formed a network to share ideas about fee-based information service, and they held the first national conference of Independent Brokers in Milwaukee in June, 1987.

The field is growing rapidly, and there will probably be a need for another conference on this topic in another two to three years rather than the five-year interval experienced this time. MITS will definitely consider sponsoring another conference when the time is right.

Notes

[1]Kathy Warye, Regional Continuing Education Program 1986–87, *Specialist: The Newsletter of Special Libraries Association*, 9, (10), October 1986, p. 2.

Targeting Your Market

Tracy M. Casorso
and Sharon J. Rogers
The George Washington University
Washington, D. C.

The investment you make in thoroughly "targeting your market" for a fee-based service will be the best investment you make while you are developing your service. "Targeting your market" is another way of saying that you are observing your environment and analyzing your organization to determine if there is a unique nexus of need and ability to serve.

The document you produce in the process of determining this need will have multiple uses. Gerre L. Jones has called marketing "the coordinating force of the 'total system' which is the service/business itself."[1] First, the document serves as a reality test for the quality of your vision about a fee-based service. Not all great ideas have validity when tested in the crucible of hard facts. A candid market study will make this clear. Second, the document will serve as an educational tool for your library and university colleagues who must understand the nature and purpose of a fee-based service in order to support and guide the task you are undertaking. Third, the marketing analysis document serves as the foundation of your overall business plan. It should help define goals and objectives.

The purpose of the presentation today is to equip you with a basic understanding of the marketing study/analysis process and the tools that are used to develop an understanding of your market. We will look at this process in three stages, devoting a section of the presentation to each:

- First, we will identify issues and concerns that should be addressed in the course of the internal analysis.
- Second, the major part of our time will focus on the market analysis itself, outlining the steps for conducting a market study.
- Third, we will suggest a format for the market planning document, including a description of an approach for segmenting and targeting the market.

The careful, thorough, and accurate conduct of a market analysis is a preliminary, rather invisible, stage of your fee-based service that may dictate its eventual success. Over eighty percent of small businesses started each year fail within five years. According to Larry Patterson of Southwest Texas State University, "many of these failures can be traced to poor planning and a vague understanding of the market to be served."[2] Fee-based services in libraries are essentially small businesses that we do not want to invest in only to have them fail. In short, a good marketing plan is a "must."

Internal Analysis

"Know thyself" is the first maxim to be observed in constructing a marketing plan. You must thoroughly know — and understand — your organization. What is it trying to achieve? What are its strengths and weaknesses? What particular opportunities are present? Which of its characteristics might threaten the success of a fee-based service?

When reviewing the aspects of your organization that will influence your development of a fee-based service, there are four key issues to be addressed:

- Will the inauguration of a fee-based service be in keeping with the overall mission of the library and of the university? Evidence is available from the university's mission statement and from the library's mission statement. You should attempt also to locate other documents at the university level to cite when justifying the service. For instance, George Washington University had a long-range planning document, a report from the Commission for the Year 2000, which contained language that was useful to identify the university's interest in a fee-based service.
- What is the library's purpose in starting a fee-based service? There are many reasons for starting such a service. The message here is that you must be honest with yourself about the real reasons. If the purpose is to increase income, it may affect the ultimate financial structuring of the institution. If the purpose is to meet external business demands for service in ways that do not conflict with the needs of current students and faculty, it may influence your choice of approaches to the market analysis itself.
- What services is the library in a position to offer? At what levels will these services be offered? Collection strengths will need to be documented. Staff expertise must be identified.
- Does the library have the resources to support a fee-based service? Will the service be priced to include a regular subsidy from the library? Does the library plan to subsidize the service for a certain number of years before it must be self-supporting or be closed? What are the commitments of space, equipment and staff? On what basis will staff be available to the service — at an hourly rate, as if they were consulting, or as part of their regularly defined "load?" How will the service interact with existing library services; for instance, will it pay a fee for reshelving journals that it uses for document delivery?

This abbreviated review of the kinds of questions that must be addressed in the internal review is expanded in the Association of College and Research Libraries (ACRL) continuing education course book, *Operating And Marketing Fee-based Services In Academic Libraries*.[3]

If "know thyself" is the maxim guiding this part of the analysis, "candor" is the watchword. Most of us are skilled at defining strengths and opportunities within our organizations. We tend to be much less honest and forthcoming about our weaknesses and the threats that these weaknesses represent. Only an objective internal profile of the organization will provide a basis for sound decision making in later stages of the marketing plan. The purpose and, indeed, the necessity of a thorough internal assessment coupled with the study of the designated market is to determine the viability of the service. If results indicate less than adequate resources or market demand, you will be saved the trouble, expense—and embarrassment—of offering the service. On the other hand, if the results show a greater demand than expected, plans can be modified accordingly.

Getting the Market Research Done

Since most libraries are not equipped with a market research unit, one of the first choices to confront is staffing the study itself. The decision, of course, is based on the time, money, and expertise at your disposal. First of all, you can do it yourself. The "cookbook" approach is an honored one which gets the job done in tight circumstances. Second, since most of us are in academic environments, your market research project may become a class project for a student or students in a course. Finally, you might choose to hire an outside consultant or marketing research firm.

Permutations of these options work too, and each approach has risks associated with it. Teaching yourself is slow and laborious. Students—even when a grade is at issue—can be remarkably casual about getting work done, or your project may be warped in some way to fit the requirements of a class. Outside consultants may be unfamiliar with an academic, non-profit environment or unfamiliar with modern libraries and information services.

The context for the internal analysis and its linkage to other parts of the market study are displayed in the following diagram (see Exhibit A). The Professional Services Marketing Matrix is adapted from a matrix used by professional design services.[4] The internal analysis we have just described in the "planning" part of the matrix and the market research we are about to describe link the internal analysis to the rest of the process of targeting a market.

The Market Study

Defining market research is like trying to define love. Products described as market research range from studies that could easily appear under the label "strategic planning" to the results of a session with a very verbose crystal ball. For our purposes, market research is a planned, organized effort to collect and analyze information for the purpose of making better marketing decisions.[5] You may make *your* definition when you do *your* study.

Marketing Studies: How to Target Your Market

Professional Services Marketing Matrix*

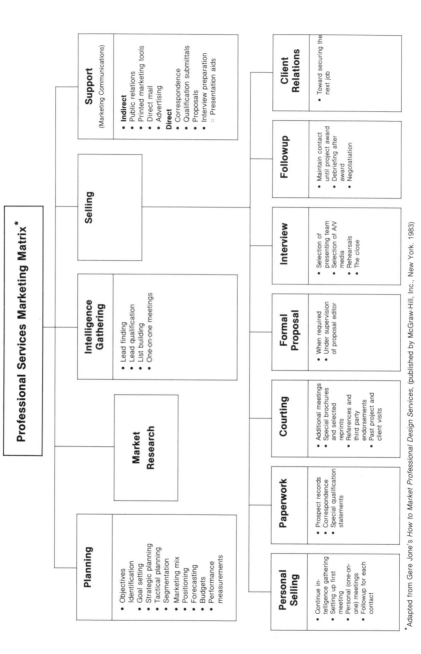

Planning
- Objectives
- Identification
- Goal setting
- Strategic planning
- Tactical planning
- Segmentation
- Marketing mix
- Positioning
- Forecasting
- Budgets
- Performance measurements

Market Research

Intelligence Gathering
- Lead finding
- Lead qualification
- List building
- One-on-one meetings

Selling

Support
(Marketing Communications)
- **Indirect**
  - Public relations
  - Printed marketing tools
  - Direct mail
  - Advertising
- **Direct**
  - Correspondence
  - Qualification submittals
  - Proposals
  - Interview preparation
    - □ Presentation aids

Personal Selling
- Continue intelligence gathering
- Setting up first meeting
- Personal (one-on-one) meetings
- Followup for each contact

Paperwork
- Prospect records
- Correspondence
- Special qualification statements

Courting
- Additional meetings
- Special brochures and selected reprints
- References and third party endorsements
- Past project and client visits

Formal Proposal
- When required
- Under supervision of proposal editor

Interview
- Selection of presenting team
- Selection of A/V media
- Rehearsals
- The close

Followup
- Maintain contact until project award
- Debriefing after award
- Negotiation

Client Relations
- Toward securing the next job

*Adapted from Gere Jone's *How to Market Professional Design Services*, (published by McGraw-Hill, Inc., New York. 1983)

4

The purpose of a market study is to develop an estimate of demand sales for a particular service/business in a specific market. A market study will determine if the potential for the desired sales volume exists in the designated market. The trauma encountered by skipping the market research stage is illustrated in the following example:

> Once there was a hospital in southern Illinois that decided to establish an Adult Day Care Center as a solution to its underutilized space. It designed a whole floor to service senior citizens who required personal care and services in an ambulatory setting during the day, but who would return home each evening. The cost was sixteen dollars a day, and transportation was to be provided by the patient's relatives. About the only research that was done on this concept was to note that a lot of elderly people lived within a three-mile radius. The Center opened with a capacity to handle thirty patients. Only two signed up![6]

Conducting a Market Study

Regardless of the method you choose for completing the market research, you will need to know the basic tasks that a market study must accomplish: defining the service, defining the trading area, and studying data on relevant characteristics of the perceived market.

When you get to the market study stage, the service must be more specifically defined than it was in the "internal analysis" stage. For instance, you decide you will offer "document delivery." Does that mean document delivery for both monographs and serials? Only from your own collection? From other collections also? A clear and specific definition of services/products will simplify the data gathering and analysis required later.

The trading area is the geographic area in which you will actually offer your services and products. The actual size of the service's geographic market is dependent upon the type of services offered and the number and location of competitors. The trading area may vary among services. For example, many fee-based services find that document delivery is both a local, national, and international market, while other services are more likely to be delivered within a more immediate geographic area.

Data collection should be both objective and efficient. Information may be obtained from both secondary and primary data sources.

Secondary data is data that has been collected for another purpose but may be adapted and analyzed for your market study; census data by postal zip code is an example. Secondary data includes internal library annual reports, public service desk statistics, and any library user studies that have been previously conducted. For instance, one element of our study at Gelman was an analysis of the levels of interlibrary loan transactions over a five year period. Other secondary sources include government publications, periodicals and books, and commercial services. Through various secondary sources you will be able to identify the firms and companies in your trading area, your competitors, and the projected growth rates for your area.[7] In another example, at George Washington University, we mapped the types and total number of firms near the university by adjacent zip codes and also presented that data in our report as a pie chart.

Primary data is data gathered for the specific purpose of the market study. Primary data collection is far more costly but must be relied upon to fill critical information gaps that cannot be met in the secondary literature. Collecting primary data allows you to test hypotheses and identify characteristics and needs relevant to your trading area.[8]

There are a number of familiar research mechanisms that may be used to gather primary data: mail surveys, questionnaires, telephone surveys, personal interviews, and panels. There are costs and benefits associated with each that are well articulated in any textbook on the subject. A variety of factors—budget, time, degree of reliability, expertise—will determine the most appropriate method to use. Whichever is selected, it must adhere to the principles of the scientific method: careful observation, formulation of hypotheses, prediction, and testing.

But at Some Point You Have to Quit

It is easy for data collection to assume a life of its own. There's always more you could know. It's particularly easy to get bogged down when we have emphasized that the entire success of your fee-based service depends on careful, thorough study.

So, at a reasonable point, you declare an end and attempt to discover if there is life after data analysis. The task begins with extrapolating the major findings from all of your data sources, finding the information that supports your major findings, presenting the findings and your recommendations. In other words, life after data analysis is defined as "getting the report done." However, the first major findings you will extrapolate are your market targets and your market segments.

Marketing Targeting and Segmentation[9]

Several concepts may be useful to understand when determining your place in a market and your approach to marketing. Mass marketing, where a seller produces, distributes, and promotes one product to all buyers is distinguished from product-differentiated marketing where a seller produces two or more products that exhibit different features, styles, quality, or size. Product-differentiated marketing is designed to offer variety to buyers rather than appealing to different market segments. Target marketing is almost the opposite of product-differentiated marketing. A seller distinguishes among many market segments, selects one or more of these segments, and develops products and marketing mixes tailored to each segment. For example, Coca-Cola developed Tab to meet the needs of diet-conscious drinkers.

Many fee-based services have engaged in target marketing even if they haven't called it that. They have recognized that their primary clients are likely to be law firms, or large corporations, or special libraries. Target marketing is designed to help sellers identify marketing opportunities more efficiently. Sellers can develop the right product for each target market, and adjust their prices, distribution channels, and advertising to reach the target market effectively. Instead of scattering their marketing effort (a "shotgun" approach), they focus it on the buyers who are likely to have the greatest purchase interest (a "rifle" approach).

Segmenting your market is the first step. Attempt to identify distinct groups who might require separate products and/or marketing mixes. There is no single way to segment a market. The researcher tries different segmentation variables, alone and in combination, hoping to find an insightful way to view the market structure. Data analysis might be based on geographic, demographic, psychological, or behavioristic variables. One variation is based on benefits sought by buyers. Benefit segmentation requires determining: 1) the major benefits that people look for in the product; 2) the kinds of people who look for each benefit; and 3) the major brands that deliver each benefit.

Your segmentation of your market will have the maximum continuing benefit if it has the following characteristics:

- measurability (degree to which size and purchasing power can be measured);
- accessibility (degree to which the segments can be effectively reached and served);
- substantiality (degree to which segments are large and/or profitable enough);
- actionability (degree to which effective programs can be formulated for attracting and serving the segments).

Finally, you decide which of the available market segments will be yours — and defend your choice — and assess its implications.

The Marketing Plan Model

Your marketing plan model is an analytical, educational, and planning tool that must be written and organized for full impact. Philip Kotler suggests a model for designing this product.[10] Exhibit B on the following page compares his ideal model with one real version that was developed at George Washington University as the proposal for its fee-based service, INQUIRE.

Conclusion

And now for the good news: a careful, thorough market plan is a good investment for one or more reasons. Once you have the process down, you will

Marketing Studies: How to Target Your Market

Sharon J. Rogers
Director of Libraries
The George Washington
University

Tracy Casorso
INQUIRE Coordinator
The George Washington
University

The Marketing Plan Model[*]
and
INQUIRE

The critical elements in a marketing plan are an executive summary with conclusions, mission statement, internal analysis, market analysis, goals and objectives, strategies, and an action plan. Below is a marketing plan model. Adjacent to the model is an outline of the course of action INQUIRE followed in the marketing planning process. Key to the INQUIRE marketing planning process is the INQUIRE PROPOSAL, a planning document presented to The George Washington University administration as justification for the institution of a fee-based research and document delivery service.

MODEL	INQUIRE
I. Executive Summary	*INQUIRE Proposal*
Summaries of the key sections of the plan	
II. Mission Statement	*INQUIRE Proposal*
Defines the service	Description of the fee-based service
III. Internal Analysis	
Strengths/Weaknesses Opportunities/Threats	Library User Study Organizational Assessment
	Commission for the Year 2000 Report The George Washington University
IV. Market Analysis	

Market Data
    Competition
    Current and New Opportunities
    Forecasts
	Market Research Survey
	Survey of Competitor
	Identified market composition
	    and market area
	Identified market characteristics

V. Marketing Program - ACTION PLAN	*INQUIRE Proposal*

Goals and Objectives
    Staffing Plan
    Strategies: Segmenting and
              Targeting the market
    Timetable
    Budget
	Marketing - Action Plan
	Business Plan
	Marketing - Action Plan
	
	Marketing - Action Plan
	Business Plan

VI. Performance Measures and Review	*INQUIRE Proposal* Business Plan

[*]Adapted from Philip Kotler's *Marketing Management: Analysis, Planning, and Control,* 5th ed. (published by Prentice-Hall, Inc., New Jersey, 1984).

Second Conference on Fee-Based Research in College and University Libraries
Ann Arbor, Michigan
May 10, 11, 12, 1987
Sponsored by The Michigan Information Transfer Source (MITS)
University of Michigan Libraries

repeat it because marketing is a dynamic, and interactive, process. Your marketing plan will be updated and reconfirmed and changed at regular intervals. It is not completed once and put on a shelf.

Notes

[1]Gerre L. Jones, *How to market professional design services*. New York: McGraw-Hill Book Co., 1983, 9.

[2]Larry T. Patterson and Charles D. McCullough, "A market study methodology for small business" *Journal of Small Business Management*, (July 1980), 31.

[3]Barbara Stump, *Operating and Marketing Fee-based Services in Academic Libraries: A Small Business Approach*. Chicago: The Association of College and Research Libraries, 1983, 15.

[4]Jones, 9.

[5]Jones, 30.

[6]Philip Kotler, Strategies for introducing marketing into non-profit organizations, *Journal of Marketing*, vol. 43, (January 1979), 37–40.

[7]Philip Kotler, *Marketing Management: Analysis, Planning and Control*, 5th ed. New Jersey: Prentice-Hall, 1984.

[8]Patterson, 34.

[9]This section owes substance and inspiration to Kotler, *Marketing Management*, 250–267.

[10]Kotler, *Marketing Management*.

Selling
the Service

Alice Sizer Warner
Information Guild
Lexington, Massachusetts

Selling Twice

A fee-based service in an academic library usually has to be sold twice. First, the university administration needs to be sold on the idea of fee-based service. Then, once the administration has given its blessing, a second kind of selling has to happen, and keep happening. That second kind of selling is of prime importance — selling to customers.

Selling to the Administration

What usually happens is that the director of the library prepares a written proposal for submission to the institution's president and governing board.

Proposals should be written clearly and lucidly, and should avoid use of library-related jargon; go-ahead decisions will be made by non-librarians. Establishment of fee-based library service should be linked to the institution's general goals, and this linkage should appear on page one of the proposal. Institutional goals might include, for instance, maintaining strong town-gown relationships or keeping in touch with alumni; a fee-based service can contribute toward both these goals by providing access to library services for these non-affiliated groups in a manner that does not sap or strain service to the primary clientele, faculty and current students.

The ideal proposal should be at most twenty double-spaced pages. It should tell you what it is going to say (usually called an "executive summary"), say what it has to say simply and clearly, and then summarize what it has said. People reading the proposal should be able to absorb it in no more than half an hour.

The body of the proposal describes the current situation, presents a fee-based service in relation to the current situation, explores goals and benefits of fee-based services, indicates who customers will be and why they will buy, and enumerates exactly what services will be offered. It is usually helpful to give brief descriptions of fee-based services in other, comparable institutions.

There will always be policy issues that need examination (such as what a fee-based service will mean to consortium members, how issues of copyright, liability, and confidentiality might be handled, and how charging fees can be reconciled with Land Grant ideals). The proposal need not give definitive solutions to all policy problems: many will be beyond the purview of the library director. The proposal should, however, indicate that these issues must be faced.

A proposal should address what will happen if *status quo* continues and a fee-based service is *not* established.

Next follows an action plan, complete with budget. It is better not to call this section a "business plan," as that phrase has different meanings for different people.

The action plan describes proposed steps in setting up the service, gives a timetable, and details what the set-up stage will cost the university. Marketing and selling plans are outlined, proposed billing rates are presented. Monthly and yearly activity goals are forecasted, as are monthly and yearly budgets.

To keep the proposal down to a twenty-page narrative, use exhibits tacked onto the end of the proposal; there need be no exhibits page limitation. Exhibits can include: university policy, library mission statement, current borrowing policies; description of market, results of any market surveys; samples of other fee-based services' brochures, disclaimer, and copyright statements; suggested wording for your fee-based service's proposed brochure, disclaimer, and copyright statements; details of start-up budget; analysis of how billing rates are being determined; activity forecasts; budget forecasts; schedules, timelines.

The library director may choose to delegate preparation of the proposal's early drafts to one or more staff members; the director may hire a consultant to help. It is the director, however, who holds final responsibility, who must defend the proposal and negotiate with institution leaders. It is to everyone's advantage that the proposal be carefully and simply prepared; the purpose is to make it very easy for the proposal to be accepted.

Selling Fee-Based Services

The person chosen to manage a fee-based service is usually the best, the hottest, reference librarian available. By definition, that person is likely to be more service oriented than sales oriented. Sales skills and techniques can be learned, yet they cannot be learned overnight. Again, by definition, the library director (who may be rusty when it comes to reference work) probably has more-than-adequate sales skills already mastered. Especially in early months, the director should be actively involved with selling, gradually turning over the responsibility as the fee-based service gains momentum and its staff learns how to sell.

The Brochure

Before the fee-based service opens, a descriptive brochure should be prepared. This is not easy. Most librarians will need help. Be sure to include:

• Name of service, name of library, name of university.

- Mailing address of service, plus information (room number, floor number) about physical location of service.
- Telephone number (be sure to include area code) as well as other communications details as applicable (Telex, Facsimile, MCI MAIL, DIALMAIL, ITT, Compuserve, The Source, etc.).
- Description of clientele who benefit from fee-based service (such as "created for organizations and individuals not affiliated with the university").
- Fee-based service specific hours of operation as well as days of the week the service is open. Is the service open whenever the library is open? Holidays, evenings, weekends?
- Explanation of rationale for fees (such as "operates on a cost-recovery, not-for-profit basis"), of when and how bills are submitted, of payment terms (such as "net fifteen days" or "net thirty days"), of how checks should be made out.
- If appropriate, description of how services can be charged to intra-university departments or projects.
- Reassurance that, while it is impossible to forecast research costs exactly, the fee-based service can give cost estimates which will not be exceeded without express client permission.
- Indication of how quickly the fee-based service can normally respond to requests, as well as description of rush service option.
- Explanation of any two-tiered fee structures (such as one fee for people currently affiliated with the university, and another for non-affiliates).
- Description of each kind of service offered (in very simple language) and schedule of fees for each kind of service.

Kinds of service might include:

— document retrieval — documents available at the library;
— document retrieval — documents not available in house which must be procured elsewhere (do not use the jargon terms "interlibrary loan" or "ILL");
— loaned books from the library's collections;
— research (fee would include an hourly fee, with a minimum — usually between one-half hour and two hours — and expenses such as database and communications charges, copyright fees, etc.);
— shipping charges (it is suggested that, rather than stating shipping charges are "at cost," a standard shipping fee be levied — this enables invoices to be enclosed with packages at time of shipment, before exact shipping charges are determined);
— rush service (often a 50–100 percent surcharge of regular service charges).

When designing a brochure, ask for critiques from people outside the library profession; the brochure must be truly self-explanatory. Avoid jargon, avoid confusion, avoid assuming that clients know, for instance, what a computer search service is. Be clear, be concise, be specific. Avoid copying other fee-based service's brochures. Fresh thinking, fresh ideas, fresh writing are best.

It is suggested that a brochure not list database vendor names or database names. These mean little to most clients and may be off-putting. A client cares most about the problem needing a solution, the question needing an answer, and not as much about processes or tools available to the librarian.

Always date fee schedules and indicate specifically how long prices will be valid. A new service almost always underprices at first; a good target date for fee reevaluation is three months after the fee-based service's opening day.

Brochures can be used in many ways; ideally, a fee-based service aims for a one-size-fits-all (i.e., all-purpose) brochure. Consider how the brochure is to be used. If a brochure is to be mailed, use a design that can accommodate a mailing label and have the printer fold the brochures. If the brochure is to be posted on bulletin boards, be sure the printer leaves some brochures *un*folded. Brochures can be enclosed with letters, so folded brochures should be small enough to fit into a regular #10 business envelope. Several fee-based services enclose a brochure with each packet delivered to a customer. If the brochure is to be handed out at meetings or conventions, determine where on the brochure a business card can be stapled.

Avoid printing large numbers of extra brochures as the first (or second or tenth) brochure attempt will probably prove unsatisfactory for any of a number of unforeseeable reasons; you do not want to be stuck with brochures that need using up before you can design another.

Selling[1]

The ideal selling world is made up of repeat customers. Repeat customers are those who authorize continuing updates on their subject of interest. Repeat customers, knowing that service is prompt, fairly priced, accurate, imaginative, reliable, timely, etc., come back again and again with new problems, with new subjects of interest. Of course a new fee-based service cannot boast repeat customers on opening day; yet a deliberate search can be made for the type of customer apt to have continuing needs.

If repeat sales are easiest sales, next easiest are sales from referral. The easiest referral is when a satisfied customer tells someone else about the service, and that someone else becomes a customer. Most referrals, however, must be actively sought: a satisfied current customer can be asked to whom else the service might sell; a contact outside the university can be consulted for five (or ten or more) ideas of individuals or companies or associations that might become clients. Learn to ask for referrals and follow up on them.

As indicated in discussing brochures, it is crucial to be absolutely clear as to what the fee-based service is selling. Explain what the fee-based service sells in words a nine-year-old will understand. Beware of library jargon. Do not use acronyms, abbreviations, or vendor names.

An example occurred recently at a two-day inventors' conference at which this author chaired sessions devoted to where and how inventors get access to information. Our panel included a university fee-based information service librarian.

We found ourselves talking about Dialog and databases, and gradually slipped into referring to "BRS" and "Lockheed," until finally an inventor in the audience put up his hand and said, "You know, I have absolutely no idea what you are talking about."

That inventor was a superb customer candidate for the fee-based information service and yet we had failed to describe what we could do for him in words that meant something to *him*, the inventor.

We backed off and explained that when computers first were invented, publishers who published fat indexes found in libraries began to use computers to alphabetize and sort and generally organize data for printing. Then, said we, publishers realized they could make extra money by letting people with terminals and telephone lines buy time on the publisher's computer databases. Databases were continually updated and people liked that.

As time went on, costs of publishing fat indexes went up, and costs of library shelves to put the printed indexes on went up, and costs of database access began to come down. Today, we explained, many indexes are not ever printed on paper, but are available only online.

We explained that our university fee-based service knew how to tie into these online indexes. The fee-based service was all set up to answer inventors' questions. "If anyone has written about what you are interested in," we explained, "we can probably find a trail of it for you. If we can't find a trail, this, too, may interest you."

Emphasizing *benefits* of using the fee-based service, rather than *processes* we librarians go through, makes sales easier. Our inventor wanted to know how he and his invention would benefit if he hired us. He didn't really care what we did as long as we could solve his problem.

When selling, the fee-based service must know exactly to whom to sell. Posting brochures on bulletin boards and waiting for customers to walk in is definitely not enough. Specifically, fee-based services must target sales efforts towards those who have money to pay the fees—preferably those customers who will come back again and again.

Who this market is varies, of course. Some fee-based services target alumni, particularly those in the lucrative professions—medicine, law, architecture, engineering, etc. Some target specific industries: automotive, environmental, or chemical, for example. Some specialize in service to government agencies.

Local businesses can be a strong market, but only if service is truly geared to serving the business community. Business people require prompt service; businesses will not become repeat customers when they find the fee-based service closed down because the librarian is at a meeting or on vacation. Businesses need prompt bills, as they may need to bill our services on to their own customers. Most business people shun fee-based services that require clients to come in for an interview.

Many fee-based services have parochial market views, looking only to their immediate environs for customers. In most cases, however, geography need not limit the customer base. Many who sell information services feel it easier to sell to distant customers than to nearby clients.

Sales Techniques

Soliciting business by mail can be very effective.

Be sure the mailing piece describes very clearly, in layman's language, exactly what services are available. The mailing might consist of an envelope containing a general brochure plus a cover letter written especially for the market being targeted (i.e., automotive-specific, inventor-specific, law-specific, etc.). The mailing might be a brochure which includes a tear-off panel-postcard which will make it easy for recipients to write for more information.

A direct mail campaign makes use of names and addresses available on labels from list brokers—check the Yellow Pages for details. Lists are available for every conceivable industry, professional or consumer group; lists can be sorted by zip code, so it is possible to define the geographical location of those who will receive the mailing. Labels generally cost a few cents each. In general, one expects two to three percent of a mailing's recipients to become customers; truly accurate forecasts come only with experience. Interestingly, if a list is used with success (however success is defined), the same list can be used again three months later and the same percentage of responses will result.

Exhibiting at professional meetings and trade shows is another sales technique. Choose the show according to the market you target: medicine, engineering, etc. The Boston Public Library's fee-based service exhibited recently at the 1987 Inventor's Show at the Boston Museum of Science; the librarian in the BPL booth emphasized patent searching capabilities, drawing much interest from show attendees as well as from inventors exhibiting in other booths.

Being listed in business-type Yellow Pages has been lucrative for some fee-based services. When considering Yellow Pages listings, remember that a fee-based service can be listed in Yellow Pages not only in your home town, but also in virtually any geographic area—for a fee. Information is available from telephone company national account representatives.

Advertising—buying space for a printed advertisement—has rarely proven to be an effective way of selling fee-based services.

Free Selling

Direct mail, exhibiting, Yellow Pages, and advertising all cost money. However, there are many free, or virtually free, ways to promote a fee-based service.

The service must be visible, which means that individuals connected with the fee-based service must be seen by, and known by, potential customers. Go to meetings of associations connected with your target market; non-members are virtually always welcome. Arrive early, introduce yourself, carry business cards and brochures. Ask for referrals, suggestions; follow up on all leads.

Make your availability as a speaker known and become known as a good speaker. Be ready to speak, even on short notice, to professional and business groups (some of which meet every week of the year). Your speech cannot be a downright hard sell. It can, however, include stories about how your customers were helped by your service. Audiences love stories and will remember them—

and you and the fee-based service. Your institution's alumni office may wish to use your speaking services at regional club meetings.

In attending meetings and giving speeches, be careful that your time is spent with groups of *customers* instead of groups of *peers* (it's only human to prefer sticking to peers rather than sticking to selling!).

Writing articles about fee-based service helps sales as long as articles are well-written, interesting, brief, to the point, and jargon-free, and are published in papers and magazines that potential customers (not other librarians) read. Ask a publication's editor if submission of an article is appropriate and adhere to suggestions about length, format, etc. A Chamber of Commerce newsletter, for instance, might be appropriate for an article on benefits of up-to-date business information, especially if specific examples can be given. Hobbyists might be reached via a mechanics magazine, alumni through a college or university's alumni magazine.

Ask Each Other

Selling is hard work. It takes many librarians a long time to like it. It takes most even longer to become good at it.

At this meeting is massed more experience to do with the in's and out's of selling fee-based information services than has probably ever before been assembled in one place.

So let us ask each other—how do you do it? what works? what doesn't work? There is much to learn here, and for many of you veteran fee-based people there is real opportunity to be of practical assistance to colleagues in other institutions.

I personally look forward to the balance of this conference, and am confident I, for one, will learn a great deal.

Thank you for including me on your program.

Note

[1]Fuller details about selling can be found in *Mind Your Own Business: A Guide for the Information Entrepreneur* NY: Neal-Schuman Publishers, 1987; see Chapter 4, Sales and Marketing, pp. 87–127.

Dollars
and Information
Services

Frances K. Wood
Program Director
Information Services Division,
Kurt F. Wendt Library, University of Wisconsin
Madison, Wisconsin

The comments in this paper are based on my personal experience as program director of a cost recovery, fee-based information service house in a land grant university library. I believe that the majority of my remarks and observations may pertain to any "information for a fee" service that is located within an *established* public, academic, or corporate library or information center.

If each person in this audience were to envision a type of information service that could feasibly be offered for a fee I have no doubt we could compile a respectable list of services. Such a list would include information services currently offered and others that definitely could be offered under the right circumstances. The list we would compile undoubtedly would contain services some of us had never considered and services we could not realistically consider offering.

If an established library or information center becomes involved in operating and managing an information service for a fee, I believe there are certain key issues that need to be decided in order that the staff in charge of the operation may know what is expected of the operation. These issues are essentially equal in importance and, depending on the particular situation, could be considered in any order; but they must all be considered.

These issues are:

1. Will the fee-based information service be a cost recovery service or will it be expected to make a profit?
2. What expenses are the fees to cover?
3. What kinds of support can be expected from the established library or information center?
4. If the information service for a fee is just starting, what funding will be made available and for what period of time? What can (and cannot) the funds be used for?

5. What provisions are there for adding new services, updating services already in place, updating equipment, additional staffing and bringing in new clients?
6. When a profit is made, who decides how the money is to be used? How can and cannot the money be used?
7. What does the administration expect from the service this year, two years from now, five years from now?

Decisions regarding these issues may change and probably will, depending on a number of factors. Outside factors that can affect decisions are new clients, clients leaving, and clients' needs changing. Internally, change factors may include more efficient ways of handling requests, new services, and new technology. Another internal change that can affect the service may be a physical relocation that positively or negatively affects workflow. A physical relocation may also affect accessibility for "walk-in" clientele. Last (but not least) the service may be affected by administrative policy changes. Establishing a fee-based information service today is somewhat different from what it was twenty-three years ago when ISD began. Fee-based information services are widely used by the business and industrial communities and are generally accepted or at least tolerated by the library community. A considerable number of established libraries and information centers have found it acceptable, feasible, and profitable, to offer information for a fee. Reasons for having a fee-based information service do vary but will probably include one or more of the following reasons:

1. A fee-based information service can be a good public relations/outreach vehicle.
2. A fee-based information service can bring in additional, needed revenue.
3. The library or information center staff, overwhelmed by outside user requests for information, need to have some of the pressure removed. (Hopefully the addition of fees may cut down on the number of requests and/or generate enough money for additional staffing)
4. Everyone, it seems, is selling information and the administration wants to get into the act.

Today, when consideration is being given to establishing a fee-based information service there is usually immediate talk of a marketing survey. A marketing survey is an excellent idea, but personally I am not aware of any established fee-based information service that has actually done one. If such a survey has been done it would be useful and interesting to find out how it was constructed, what areas were surveyed, how the results were used by the administration underwriting the survey, and whether or not the people in charge felt the end results were worthwhile. After discussing surveys with the University of Wisconsin-Madison Survey Research Laboratory personnel, I think a market survey can be a very useful tool, but it is important to get professional assistance in its construction.

For our purposes here, let us assume the administration has determined the library or information center can provide a service or services that someone will be willing to pay for, and decisions have been reached in regard to the key issues mentioned earlier. Before advertising and promoting these services there

20

are policy decisions that should be made. These policy decisions, like the key issues, will be subject to changes and revisions.

Some of the policy decisions that can affect the cost of providing services are:

1. Who will be your clientele? Will there be a different fee structure for members and non-members, clients with deposit accounts, residents or non-residents? Remember, price breaks are nice gestures, but price variations for the same service will increase record-keeping time.
2. Will the service be limited to information available only on-site?
3. Will the information-for-a-fee service have ready and easy access to the available on-site information?
4. What provision will there be for staffing? An ideal information service, based on using on-site library material, will require a staff that knows the collection as well as outside resources, understands and speaks "libraryese," and can relate to a public that is not conversant in library and/or academic terminology.
5. If document delivery is one of the services being offered, what is the time frame for delivery? What is considered rush service? How much additional staff time will be involved in processing a rush request? What level of staff personnel will be involved?
6. If the library or information center is located in a state that has sales tax, will any or all of the services offered require the added sales tax?
7. What records will need to be kept? What or who will determine this? What formats are available and acceptable? For how long a period will the records need to be kept? Will the storage area be reasonably accessible?
8. What statistics will be kept, and for what purpose?
9. The form and format in which requests are submitted will make a difference in the time involved in processing a request. Will this affect the pricing policy?
10. How much space will be alloted for the information service? Will there be provision for walk-in clients? Will there be space set aside for working with on-site clients? Will the service have its own telephone number?
11. How often will invoices be sent? How soon will payment be due? Will the client be penalized for late payment? If detailed invoicing is needed by the client, will there be an additional charge? How are unpaid invoices to be handled?

These questions represent a small cross-section of the kind of decisions ISD has made over the years.[1]

It is generally recognized as good business procedure for an information service such as we are here concerned with, to capitalize on its establishment's strengths and to offer services accordingly. Consequently, an information service is highly dependent upon the collection and the good will and cooperation of establishment staff.

It should be recognized, moreover, that an information service is a labor-intensive operation. Material may be available on-site, but someone has to identify it, "pull it," organize it, prepare it for delivery, and record whatever details are necessary for determining costs and invoicing. It may cost five or ten cents to photocopy a page of information, but the labor—the time involved in logging in the request, locating the material, copying, closing the log, and arranging for delivery of that page — certainly add to the cost.

Let us consider that photocopy of that one page of information, and to keep the processing of the request as simple as possible let us assume the request is correctly cited on a correctly filled and separated ALA form. An ISD flowchart shows there are twenty-two procedures that need to be done by a clerk and student help before that simple request is ready for mailing. During ISD's early years, and even today, we take a specific service and follow it through, in an attempt to simplify and combine procedures, to determine whether the procedures are being performed at the proper level, how much time is involved, and whether or not charges for the service recover costs.

Approximately forty-one percent of the ISD budget is used for classified and unclassified salaries and student wages. University policy requires adding an additional twenty-nine percent to salaries to help defray costs for such fringe benefits as vacations, sick leave, and medical insurance. The ISD staff is made up of myself (full time), a three-quarter time reference librarian, a full time clerk, a one-third time fiscal clerk and the equivalent of eighty hours per week in student help. The reference librarian and the fiscal clerk are actually full time positions which are shared with the Kurt F. Wendt Library.

ISD also has an arrangement with Computerized Bibliographic Services (CBS) located within the Wendt Library. ISD is charged by CBS for staff and search time on a cost recovery basis and also includes record keeping involved in doing searches. ISD receives the searches ready for delivery. ISD and CBS staff collaborate on determining databases to be searched and terms to be used, but ISD is responsible for the searches. ISD also uses CBS staff expertise to write simple computer programs for runs of mailing labels, dialing into outside sources, etc.

Approximately fifty-five percent of ISD's budget is spent on supplies and services. This is a broad category that includes a wide spectrum of supplies necessary for the operation of an efficient labor-intensive office. ISD requisitions for all supplies and such services as on-line searching, foreign patents, and other materials not available on campus are processed through the Wendt Library business office. The office processes the requisitions, keeps records, and follows through to be certain ISD accounts are accurately posted by the University of Wisconsin business office. The remaining four percent of ISD budget is set aside for new capital equipment, replacement, or repairs.

Operating an information service costs money. Like any business, an information service business requires staff, equipment, and supplies. Substantial sums of money may need to be paid out before clients are invoiced or invoices are paid. Operating a fee-based information service within an established library or information center has many advantages in addition to being close to where the information is located. If CBS services and record keeping by the Wendt business office were done by ISD, an additional forty to sixty hours of staff time would be needed.

In addition to the expertise on the Wendt Library staff ISD has access to the support and expertise of some 120 campus librarians in forty-two other libraries and information centers. There is excellent rapport between ISD and campus librarians. It is important to note here how gratifying it is to be so well accepted, and ISD tries not to abuse privileges and to reciprocate however we can. Without this kind of support and rapport it would be much more difficult to operate, even with additional staffing.

There are numerous other benefits to be gained from operating within an established organization. For example, the University of Wisconsin central business office has been and is very helpful in assisting ISD to follow both University and state rules and regulations regarding invoicing and payments. The central business office receives all payments made to ISD, deposits the checks and sends ISD a monthly statement reflecting invoices paid. When ISD was setting up its operation, the central business office provided us with information regarding University regulations, Wisconsin sales tax, record retention, invoice formatting, and collection procedures. In the event that a collection agency is needed, the central office will handle it for us.

This paper has outlined the key areas that are important for controlling costs and establishing criteria for fees and services. I sincerely hope this overview will prove useful to you if you are beginning a fee-based service or if you're evaluating a fee-based service that is already in operation.

Note

[1]See also, Checklist Prepared to Assist Libraries Considering Fee-Based Reference Service, *RASD Update*, 8 (1), January/March 1987, pp. 3–4.

Information Brokerage: The View from the Private Sector

J. Michael Homan
Corporate Technical Library
The Upjohn Company
Kalamazoo, Michigan

Special libraries in industry such as Upjohn's Corporate Technical Library are dedicated to serving a special clientele with a balanced mix of services that offer a competitive advantage to the corporation in a cost-effective way. Products and services offered by fee-based information services complement those that are performed in-house with company resources, often extending a lean staff or providing a resource otherwise unavailable internally. This paper will review reasons for using fee-based information services, using examples from the Upjohn environment, and discuss a number of important issues from the perspective of a corporate special library.

The Upjohn Library System Overview

The Upjohn Company is a worldwide, research-based producer and marketer of pharmaceuticals, health care services, fine chemicals, seed and agricultural specialties. Kalamazoo, Michigan serves as the corporate, research, and medical headquarters. There are some 22,000 employees worldwide; about 8,000 are employed in Kalamazoo. The Upjohn Library System consists of the Corporate Technical Library, the Business Library and the Medical Library Services unit, together with a number of unit or departmental collections in Kalamazoo, plus overseas subsidiary collections and information services. My comments about fee-based services are derived from the experiences of the Corporate Technical Library.

The Corporate Technical Library (CTL) has a staff of thirty-nine including eighteen information professionals and twenty-one office staff. The CTL provides various technical and information services common to most libraries such as cataloging and computer based literature searching and, in addition, has responsibility for research records management and the corporate information systems related to published information about the company's products and internally generated proprietary information (primarily technical reports). The

CTL is a fully automated library through the integrated library automation system, LIS (Library Information System), which includes a corporate online catalog.

Make or Buy

Using internal resources to produce a product or service versus buying the product or service externally is the "make or buy" decision faced by all information managers. Examples of make or buy decisions where the decision was to buy externally are probably easy to come by in any organization. In the library world most institutions do relatively little original cataloging, preferring to buy access to electronic catalog records or card producing services from various information utilities such as OCLC (Online Catalog Library Center). Journal binding and journal subscription services are other examples of services purchased from external service bureaus. The CTL uses fee-based services for a great variety of services and products. A list of information services supplied by external service bureaus appears in Figure 1.

We have three resource options available to us when we want to offer a product or service: 1) use our own internal (CTL) resources; 2) purchase the product or service from another Upjohn service unit; or 3) purchase externally. We use fee-based information services on a selective basis when there are clear reasons for doing so. The reasons include cost-benefits derived, competitive advantage to the company, project control, resource availability, and convenience. Some Upjohn illustrative examples follow.

Cost-Benefits Derived

Cost-benefits from using contract services may include a faster turnaround time for processing materials or potential salary savings from the use of contract labor for special projects. When compared to the cost of purchasing a larger journal collection, the cost of purchasing documents from document vendors is very competitive with what it would cost to provide this service internally. Although resources are expended on quality control for each service purchased externally, benefits are obtained by conserving head count in a highly controlled head count environment. Internal resources are also conserved by eliminating the need for personnel recruitment, training, and supervision.

The use of OCLC in our environment for obtaining shared catalog records is the obvious technical services example. An example of fee-based information services is our use of a service bureau to build a database of published scientific literature on Upjohn products. The CTL is responsible for a published product literature monitoring system called PIRSU (Product Information Retrieval System/Upjohn). PIRSU is the corporate information management system for computer-assisted documentation and retrieval of published literature dealing with the company's pharmaceutical, veterinary and agricultural products. For more than ten years the CTL has used a service bureau for literature scanning, indexing, and database construction. The major cost-benefits derived from using a service bureau for database construction rather than inhouse staff has been the ability to use professional inhouse staff for a much greater mix of information services as well as expanded services in the areas of online literature searching, current literature alerting, end-user online training, information management consulting, and reference.

Competitive Advantage

The pharmaceutical industry is both highly competitive and highly regulated. The right information supplied at the right time can provide a significant competitive advantage by increasing productivity and decreasing the time that a product takes to make it from the laboratory to the market. The decision to use a contract service rather than provide it inhouse may offer a competitive advantage to the company, although this may be difficult to measure accurately in all instances.

Timely delivery of the results of literature research is one of our primary goals. Off-loading certain categories of literature research requests to fee-based services can significantly affect the turnaround time on high priority projects we complete inhouse. Providing a client with an analyzed literature research report where several online files may have been merged, sorted and duplicate citations eliminated, or highly relevant citations highlighted, decreases the time it takes a client to review and digest the results of the literature search. Our inhouse staff can produce a larger number of analyzed reports for high priority projects or initiate new services more frequently when we have the flexibility of using fee-based information services. Contracting out selected literature research projects also helps smooth out the frequent peaks and valleys common to service organizations resulting from various external factors such as rush projects, staff vacations, and staff professional leaves.

In a sense, "farming out" the product literature scanning, indexing and database construction project offers a competitive advantage by expanding our capability to provide various information services such as online literature searching and current literature alerting. Our capability for providing such services is undoubtedly greater than competitor companies whose information departments are still completely saddled with internal database construction.

Project Control

Competing internal priorities will sometimes force the issue of make or buy as was the case with the online database component of the PIRSU product literature information system. The PIRSU online database is mounted as a private database at a timesharing vendor. At the time we initiated our private database service we had greater control over the update schedule, software modifications, error corrections, and other issues related to bibliographic databases than had been possible when the database was mounted internally. This was due primarily to competing priorities of our internal mainframe operation. Another important issue in deciding to buy externally was the value-added advantage of sophisticated retrieval software and worldwide telecommunications access offered by the timesharing vendor which were not available internally at the time. We currently derive many additional value-added benefits from the private database contract including attractive rates on publically available databases and a high-speed mainframe-to-mainframe communications network link between our Research Computer Center and the vendor mainframe.

Resource Availability

Products or services not available internally include documents which we purchase from document vendors and the services of professional staff for indexing and abstracting.

Copies of published documents are supplied on demand by CTL document delivery staff using the collections of the Library or various external sources. Although we subscribe to approximately 1,500 scientific journals and monographic series which are carefully selected to match the literature needs of the drug development process at Upjohn, there is a great need for obtaining items we do not hold from external document vendors. We filled approximately 47,000 document requests (primarily journal articles) in 1986. Over 16,000 of these requests (34 percent) were purchased from outside sources.

The CTL has responsibility for the corporate information management system for internal proprietary literature. This system parallels the PIRSU system for published product literature, but is maintained on an in-house mainframe. The current volume of internal proprietary documents being written exceeds our capacity to index and abstract these items on a timely basis using currently allocated full-time staff. We are therefore using an information service bureau to supply local contract indexers and abstractors for our proprietary information system. Our contract staff work in-house under close supervision and, of course, sign a statement of confidentiality regarding the proprietary documents they handle. The issue of confidentiality precluded our use of a service bureau to index and abstract proprietary documents at a location external to the company.

Convenience

One of the information services the CTL provides is online training for end-users on biomedical, chemical, and internal databases. Although we use our own staff to train users on internal databases, we have found it convenient to bring in trainers from selected external systems or databases such as the STN

International system (bibliographic and registry files in chemistry) and various BRS biomedical databases. Our in-house staff could have put together a training program for each of the databases on which we offer training, but we chose to use the established and tested training services of the database producers or vendors for the sake of convenience.

Issues in Using Fee-Based Services

Once a decision is made to buy an information service or product externally, other issues related to cost, standards, quality control, communication, and the ability to meet special needs come into play.

Cost

We want to offer the best mix of information services in the most cost-effective way. Our mix of services includes internal services that our full-time staff provides and services or products that we have decided to purchase externally based on the various reasons previously discussed. The service bureau that provides the best service at a competitive cost will get our business. Providing the best service relates to the issues of standards, quality control, communication, and the ability to meet special needs discussed below.

Standards

Our in-house efforts to meet our customers' information needs are based on a sense of urgency, accurateness, and cost-effectiveness. Service bureaus which supply fee-based information are expected to meet standards related to these same areas together with confidentiality. A service-bureau-supplied product such as a literature search or fact retrieval answer should match the same quality, timeliness, and accuracy our customers have come to expect of our own internally supplied services.

Quality Control

Services or products supplied to us from a service bureau require a quality control program at our end to monitor how well the service bureau is performing. Quality control, although partially automated in our environment for some services, remains a highly labor-intensive operation and critical to the successful use of fee-based services. Before we can even consider a fee-based service we must work out quality control procedures and have the internal staff resources to monitor the quality of the service being provided externally. We expect a service bureau to have a specific quality control program in place for each service supplied.

Communication

Timely and regular two-way communication with a service bureau helps maintain the appropriate rapport essential for a good business relationship. This includes prompt follow-up and resolution of billing errors, miscommunication, etc. Quality control feedback loops from client to service bureau help facilitate the communication process by letting a contractor know where he stands and what areas should be improved.

Ability to Meet Special Needs

Last but not least is the ability of a fee-based service to meet special needs and relate to our organization with sincere respect and goodwill.

All organizations have different internal procedures, policies, and special needs. We expect fee-based services to respect this fact and have the flexibility to meet our requirements (within reason, of course). For example, we ask service bureaus supplying literature searches to use an Upjohn form to record the search formulation executed, databases searched, and the time spent on each phase of the search including formulation time, online time, and edit time. Service bureaus supplying documents are expected to handle handwritten, often unverified, photocopy requisition forms submitted by our clients.

Phrases like "treatment of individuals with respect and dignity in all communications," "giving a client the benefit of the doubt," "generation of goodwill," and "showing a genuine interest in a client's business" may all sound trite, but nonetheless are very important concepts in the maintenance of successful, longstanding business relationships. We look for fee-based organizations which meet these intangible criteria.

Conclusion

Our organization has successfully used fee-based information services for a variety of services and products over a long period of time. We have been able to extend a lean staff and provide resources not available internally. The use of fee-based services has strengthened our operation by giving it the flexibility to respond quickly and effectively to ever-changing corporate priorities. Advances in technology have helped us implement more sophisticated quality control measures; competition among service bureaus has helped keep costs at a reasonable level. Generally speaking, the use of fee-based services has made good business sense for our current operation.

The activities of the professional staff at many corporate libraries are evolving. The activities of information management consulting and online training are becoming routine activities. Our ideal future scenario includes greater professional staff involvement with drug and product development teams and the provision of synthesized information products. As we evolve toward our ideal future, the use of fee-based services will help us meet our continuing obligation for the type of services we have always provided and which are still very much in demand, and give us the flexibility to investigate new and improved information services for the future.

Quality Control in Fee-Based Library Services: Who Cares?

Elizabeth Lunden
Director of the Learning Resource Center
North Harris County College
Houston, Texas

When you buy a product or service on the market you expect certain things of it. You become concerned if these expectations are not met. As a consumer you have a right to expect that the product will function as advertised; that it will last for a reasonable length of time; that it satisfies your needs; that you are able to get it when you need it. Frequently, you are even willing to pay a little extra to assure the above conditions. Depending on the importance or expense of the product or service, you may take the time to study the market and shop around for what you think is the best product or service available and the best dealer from which to buy it.

If your selection doesn't meet your expectations you may do several things about it almost always including griping to your friends, colleagues, and anyone else that will listen, and complaining to the manufacturer or the seller to try to correct the situation. Why? Because you needed it, you selected it from among alternatives, you paid for it, and it did not satisfy your expectations.

The manufacturer or seller, if he receives enough of this type of feedback, understands that if he wants to remain in business, he must correct the problems. We have become a very quality-conscious nation of consumers, and the word "quality" is predominant in consumer information, advertising, and ultimately in business management circles. There is no end to the management theories, techniques, and fads relating to quality control in the business literature. The reason is user expectations. When the clients have high expectations and really care, that is the genesis of quality control.

A fee based service in an academic library can be the best of both worlds. In a sense you are putting your library service on the line and testing the quality of it, by charging for it. Your employees must understand that they no longer work in a library. A fee-based service is a business. The clients have high expectations, they care, and they want quality work.

Characteristics of a Quality Product

In order to assess quality control we must first develop a clear definition of quality in relation to our unique product. When you think in terms of how effective your product is, you can narrow the important characteristics of quality down to specific attributes. Once you have been in business for awhile, it is a useful exercise to fully analyze your product in terms of a few clearly defined quality criteria. This presentation will provide a framework for evaluating your services in terms of quality and for taking steps to control that quality. For our definition I submit the following list of appropriate quality criteria:

1. **Accuracy.** Is the information factually correct?
2. **Appropriateness.** Is the answer thorough and does it clearly respond directly to the client's needs?
3. **Timeliness.** Is your turnaround time routinely prompt, and can you accommodate special deadlines?
4. **Absence of Errors.** From receipt of the request all the way through to the billing process, is the total product completely without error; i.e., are all parts and pages there; is everything legible and spelled correctly; is the billing information correct?
5. **Consistency.** Can the client expect the same level of service all the time, no matter whom he talks to, what time of day it is, or what time of the year it is? Or are the consistency and reliability of your service subject to many variables?
6. **Image.** The client's perception of quality is often based on image and appearance. Appearance of the product, the bill, the office environment, and the staff play an important part in the image aspects of quality, as do telephone manners and the ease of communication between client and company. If your image does not project quality, the client will not perceive that he is receiving a quality service.

Factors That Affect Quality

Once you have identified the criteria that you will use to judge the quality of your product you may be able to select for priority attention those areas that seem to be your weakest: for example, too many errors or poor response time. The next step is to list all of the factors that seem to affect that particular aspect of quality. I will suggest a few examples for each criterion of quality that we have identified.

Accuracy

Some aspects of quality rely on the intellectual input of the individual working on the request. Accuracy is certainly one of these aspects. Accuracy depends mainly on two things. The first is human input, especially the interpretive judgment that must be added, such as relationships between the data or the application of formulas and calculations. Equally as important is the reliability of the sources used to answer the question. Not only must they be expert sources, but they also must be the most current available. Answers are only as good as the sources, whether these are print sources, databases, or even human resources. These sources, as well as any judgments or analyses that are added, should be cited to the client. The transcription and relaying of the information to the client is also a factor in providing accurate answers.

Appropriateness

Both accuracy and appropriateness of the answer are important factors when answering reference questions, and appropriateness is even more important when designing and performing database searches for a client. While an answer may be absolutely accurate, it is worthless unless it responds directly to the question asked by the client. The intellectual side here emerges from a slightly different perspective. Quality in this case depends more on the client interview, and on the two-way communication, to determine exactly what it is that the client needs to know. Background information elicited from the client is crucial, as is the background knowledge or experience brought to the question by the staff member. Knowledge and selection of resources, and the design and structure of database searching are other ways that the human input will affect the appropriateness of your responses. Sources, too, are the other half of the question, but in this case the question is not so much the reliability but instead the availability of the sources. What kinds of resources are available to you to answer the question, and how much time are you willing to invest to identify and obtain sources that respond directly to the client's needs? Close, in this case, is not close enough.

Timeliness

Much less intellectual in nature, the issue of timeliness usually depends on more tangible, but not necessarily more easily controlled factors. Many things affect how quickly a request can be processed and returned to the client. If a client does not receive the response when requested, however, this issue can become your most important quality problem. Things that may affect timeliness include the following: client interview and a clear understanding and communication of when the response is needed and the options available to the client; the availability and reliability of a variety of delivery options, including the mail; institutional factors such as on-campus handling of mail, packages, and special delivery services (since not everyone has the same sense of urgency that you do); your policy regarding the use of the telephone in accepting requests, providing answers, and maintaining contact about delays and deadlines; immediate availability of resources; equipment malfunctions; availability of staff and staff backup systems; organizational considerations such as the handling of routine vs. special rush requests, or the handling of very difficult vs. standard requests; and identification and ability to respond to backlogs while maintaining a smooth work flow.

Absence of Errors

This may be the most difficult to control, because it depends not so much on intellectual input or on physical things, but more on human variables. Errors can usually be traced to three causes. They may be procedural or systemic in nature; they may occur as a result of inadequate training; they may occur simply as a result of carelessness or lack of attention to detail. Errors, more than any other aspect of quality, must be traced to their source because the cause has to be identified in order to avoid continuous repetition. This can be intimidating to staff, but an explanation of the reason for constant vigilance, as well as involvement of the staff in catching errors will make the process seem less threatening. An immediate benefit will be fewer errors, as a result of the extra attention given to the problem. Such things as correct transcription of client interviews; clear handwriting; across the board understanding of both routine and new procedures; systems that work; boredom and lack of variety on the job; office environment; pressures caused by backlogs, and perceived emphasis on quantity vs. quality; and accurate maintenance of client records can all contribute to the error level that will be a characteristic of the quality of your product.

Consistency

This is an issue that depends more on client perception but it is based on very real factors. Quality service will be perceived as a service that is consistently good in every respect, not something that varies depending on who you talk to, who works on the request, and what time of year it is. Consistency depends on staff availability no matter who is sick or what time of year it is; established routines; thorough training of staff; "routine" responses to non-routine situations; the ability and willingness of the staff to communicate with each other; absence of ego, which results in a sharing of staff expertise; and attention to all other aspects of quality control.

Image

Much depends on the perception of the client when evaluating the quality of a service they use. To a large degree this perception is affected by the feeling that if something looks good, sounds good, and is easy to use, then it must be good. If you pay attention to these characteristics, then you may be perceived to give as careful attention to the work you perform. Of course you must back up this image with a good product. A negative image will almost certainly inspire very low expectations on the part of the client, which they will inevitably perceive to be fulfilled. In order to project the appropriate image to a client, you must analyze what values are held by the client, remembering that they are part of the business world and not the academic world. Efficiency is one of these values. Being able to communicate with a client in a friendly but efficient manner, with limited socializing, is an example of this. Your staff should project a comfortable appearance but be neat and businesslike, especially those staff members that will interact with clients. The working environment should give the impression of being organized, and not frantic. Your stationery, business cards, brochures, newsletters and all other mailings must reflect the standards of the business world. Furthermore, the pride that your own staff has in the image of the organization will be reflected in the results of their day-to-day effort.

Control of Quality

We have defined quality. We have determined a variety of factors that affect quality. You can approach control of quality in one of two ways. You might select an aspect of quality that demands priority attention in your service, and work on it until you trace it to all of the sources of the problem; or you might address all of the potential sources of problems equally with the hoped-for result that no specific quality problem will ever emerge. Potential problems do not become real problems until something goes wrong, so your task is to anticipate everything that can go wrong and maximize your efforts in each area. A single problem will affect several areas of quality. These may include problems such as staffing, training, procedures, environment, and external factors. No matter what aspect of quality you focus on, and no matter what factors you determine are contributing to your weakness in that area, the fundamental issues will be the same.

Availability of Resources

The variety and availability of resources affect several aspects of our definition of quality, most notably accuracy, appropriateness, and timeliness. Since you are in an academic setting with an existing collection, in a sense the resources available to you are predetermined: you will have little influence in the collection development department if you ask for materials that will be more helpful to your area than to the general curriculum. One of the controls you do have, however, is in the selection of the products you will offer and the identification of your particular market segment. If oil and petroleum are the specialities of your school, you can choose to market products to that segment locally and nationally. If certain materials are very important to your product line, you may be able to choose to purchase them for your department, or for the general collection. You can develop special access to identifiable collections that complement your own, in other institutions throughout the country, or locally. Special cooperative fast service arrangements with other fee-based services such as the new electronic mail network of the FISCAL (Fee-based Information Service Centers in Academic Libraries) Discussion Group in ALA; the use of runners or contacts on your payroll in other institutions; participation in special networks and courier services with other local institutions; and other methods of identifying and accessing complementary collections should be explored. Do not overlook human resources including your own institution faculty, personal contacts with authors of published or unpublished papers, government agencies, or firms that may sell the information that you are seeking. Aggressive use of the telephone and letters to primary sources, and in the development of personal contacts or expediters in key libraries and institutions, will greatly expand the resources available to you and help to improve quality in the areas of availability, accuracy, and timeliness.

Procedures

Procedures usually affect timeliness, error control, and consistency. If procedures seem to be at the heart of your quality problem, you must carefully examine each procedure related to the problem. The first and maybe the most important step is to discuss that particular procedure with the staff involved.

35

Here we take a lesson from the Japanese and form an ad hoc quality circle to address the problems and propose solutions. Getting the staff involved creates a form of commitment by making them highly aware of the quality problem, and this in itself may result in more care in the execution of the procedure. Another benefit of staff contribution to the development of procedures is staff involvement in the resolution of the procedure problem and their resulting feeling of ownership in procedural changes and interest in making the procedure work. This should result in greater attention to detail and the important ongoing feedback regarding the effectiveness of the procedure.

Procedure manuals, preferably done on a word processor, are crucial as a training device, as an immediate reference for a refresher on a procedure, and as an historical record of "the way we've always done it." They are invaluable as a reference when quality problems arise. The creation of a procedures manual, if done with staff interview as part of the process, will immediately identify divergent interpretations of procedures. Specific pages for individual procedures may be duplicated and kept handy in appropriate work areas to be used by staff as a quick reference, especially if those tasks are not regularly performed by that staff member. This is much easier than expecting staff (especially when someone is working in an unfamiliar way) to "ask someone" or to search for a procedure in an entire procedures manual, which may be too much of a barrier to the access of the necessary information. The alternative of "faking it" will be too tempting.

When someone on your staff leaves, you need to provide plenty of time for "debriefing." During this process the individual should review his procedures in the manual, and update them with notations for suggestions for improvement, or hints in the practical application of procedures. In fact, you shouldn't wait for staff to leave to do this.

Faulty systems and procedures are a major component of error control and are one of the three key causes of errors.

Training

Another component of error control is training of staff. When you first identify errors as one of your quality problems, you probably should suspect training first. This also provides you with the opportunity to discuss it with staff in a less threatening context.

Training must be done both verbally and in writing, and new staff must be carefully monitored during an initial period, with immediate feedback. While monitoring should be done by all staff related to that particular task, with the side benefit of involving staff in the control of quality, feedback should only be given by the supervisor.

Prior to training on a specific job, new employees should be provided with an orientation to the entire operation and the institutional setting and a clear understanding of where their task fits in. A mixture of training and orientation will minimize confusion on the part of the employee.

A written step by step training procedure must be developed and closely followed for each position. Training is too important to be left to the inclinations of the person doing the training and to improvised responses to "on the job" situations. The step by step training manual is for the supervisor, not for the employee. The procedures manual is for the employee.

Personnel

The mechanics of personnel is probably one of the key causes of every problem with quality control but especially in the areas of timeliness, error control, and consistency. Specific problems include the availability of sufficient personnel at all times; development of backup systems; the use of student assistants; and prompt hiring of new staff members. Often there is not a lot that can be done because it is controlled by your institutional system — which can be notoriously slow at times. In the event of a short term personnel shortage, sickness or vacation, for example, all staff must be made aware of the immediate priorities so that each is working with common goals in mind. This will contribute to teamwork in handling the time of "crisis." Back up systems must be in place so that staff have both a primary and a secondary job on which they are trained. This can be accomplished by deliberate job switching in advance so that staff is trained in more than one task. This has the added benefit of changing routine and gaining staff involvement. Trained temporary help, or at least help that is familiar with your operation, can be invaluable in resolving personnel shortages. This might be arranged by borrowing from elsewhere within the library, or through a moonlighting arrangement if allowed; by using librarians from other local institutions for temporary part time work; or by expanding the hours of your own part time staff.

The availability of student assistants is a mixed blessing. The fact that they are less expensive is in their favor. They may be, however, prone to error due to lack of true commitment or to insufficient training due to their transient nature. They can be unreliable because of academic and social pressures; their first priority is being a student. They are not necessarily subject to a formal evaluation system. Some of these problems can be counteracted by a concerted effort at training and attempts to get them involved in the goals of the organization. Specialization of tasks makes training easier by giving them a single area to learn well. It is important, however, not to place them in an area that is so specialized that no one else is really familiar with the procedure or to place them in a position that demands daily attention. A modified system of evaluation for student assistants can be utilized to promote the positive and correct the problems. One solution of the student assistant problem is to consolidate most of the funds available for student assistants and use the funds to hire regular part-time staff who do not bring with them so many of the potential disadvantages of student assistants. Cutting down on the number of student assistants will reduce your supervisory problems, and you will find that regular part time staff can learn more and accomplish more than several student assistants.

Communication

Communication among your staff about the product is critical to controlling the quality of the product, especially in such areas as accuracy and appropriateness. There can be no room for egos in this type of organization, and a system should be established that promotes communication and sharing of information. A regular "quality circle" meeting among staff members of like tasks for the purpose of sharing information, problems, and sources should be established. It must be built into the system that your staff will seek each other's assistance. The whole in this case is greater than the individual parts. A fresh point of view, a different kind of background and experience, and new ideas on resources are invaluable. Additionally the best of everyone's Rolodex must be consolidated into a central information bank accessible to all staff and shared at meetings. Again, the debriefing of departing staff is vital to this process.

Open two-way communication must also consistently take place between the supervisor of each task and the employees performing the task to assure an awareness of and response to specific problems, procedures, and new ideas which affect timeliness, and consistency. This helps keep the team involved at all times.

Commitment

Staff commitment affects all aspects of quality control because you are only as good as your team. Development of staff commitment to the goals of your organization is different from the mechanics of your personnel problems. Pride and involvement are the keys here, as well as reward. You can increase involvement by sharing with the staff certain statistics which could be considered key indicators of how well you are doing. Specifically this might include the monthly number of incoming requests, the number of document requests filled, the number of new accounts, and the number of cancelled requests. Financial information is not necessary. I found it effective to set tangible goals of quantity for the staff as a whole. In fact if we reached a certain number of document requests completed for each month, I would personally treat the entire staff to lunch. It became a tangible goal and the extra effort was evident because the reward was both attainable and fun. Quality was built into this system because if we were not doing a good job, our clients, who are business people and librarians, would find another way to get their work done. In this world there is competition. We are by no means a monopoly.

Staff involvement will result in staff commitment. Be sure the whole staff is involved in whatever quality problem you are working to resolve, whether it is speed, error control, image building, etc. If you have supervisory layers, have each supervisor work with their own staff, including student assistants. Job switching (as we have previously mentioned) has several benefits, including increasing involvement, relieving monotony and thereby reducing errors, and providing trained backups in key positions to help you address the problems of staff shortages or backlogs. Often just focusing on a problem will result in some improvement of the situation, because the staff involved will become aware of the problem, and will become more attentive to the process.

Part of the reward to staff for working in any organization should be the opportunity for personal development. This should be a concern of the supervisors and of the line staff. The success of such an organization often depends on interpersonal relations. Training films or presentations from outside (possibly your counseling office) on teamwork, stress management, telephone manners, and time management, for example, will communicate personal development information to your staff from an objective source, will help you contribute to their development, and may resolve some problems or prevent potential problems in your department.

Of course it is imperative that any compliments received from clients, or from anywhere, must be shared with the whole staff.

Equipment

The equipment that you use may be part of your quality problem, but may not be easily resolved due to expense or availability. For instance, if speed is one of your quality problems, you may want to look into a telefax machine, either for receiving pages of requests, for sending information to your clients, or perhaps through cooperative arrangements with suppliers, achieving faster turnaround on documents that you request from other sources.

Computers may resolve myriad quality problems associated with keeping track of progress on various requests, producing and updating training and procedures manuals and files of resources, and maintaining your accounting files, which can also be updated with new client information. Database searches done on a computer using wordprocessing produces a professional looking print product which will enhance your quality image.

The quality of your product can be affected by the quality of your photocopy equipment. Usually we must do the best we can with what we have, but photocopy quality will affect your image as well as the readability of the product. Tightly bound journals are a problem, and I do wonder if the new copying product that is hand held and will copy a three inch wide strip of a page will help with those tight bindings.

An important aspect of the equipment consideration is service. Equipment is only good when it is working, and your timeliness and consistency requires dependable equipment and prompt servicing.

Environment

The working environment will affect almost every aspect of quality of the product. An organized office with a smooth work flow will impact both the efficiency and the accuracy with which a request is handled. A quiet, calm working environment, free from distractions and interruptions, will be more conducive to everyone's best effort. Also essential is a quiet private area where quality meetings can be held or difficult problems reviewed. Enough room so that everyone has an area they feel is their own will affect staff involvement and ultimately the quality of the product. A neat environment will project a businesslike image to visiting clients.

So How Do We Know?

The most important thing to remember about quality is that the only real judge of your quality is the client. This is a business, and the client does indeed care. Remember that all of your clients are individuals and each has special needs. What is an important quality consideration for one may not be for another, and even these may change over time.

As important as your own internal control of quality problems is your ability to *detect* your quality problems. Since the clients have expectations, they will assess every product they receive from you in terms of those expectations. Some times they will give feedback to you. More often they will give it to their own colleagues. They will not talk about the routinely good things, but you can be sure they will talk about the occasional lapses. The answer is to be so good that an error or problem will seem exceptional to your clients and give them something positive to talk about. You do need to systematically assess how well you are doing, and preferably to have your clients know that you are concerned. One excellent method for accomplishing this is the advisory board, made up of a cross section of clients, whose job it may be to provide feedback on every aspect of the operation. You should make it a point to request their feedback on the specific aspects of quality as we have defined it.

The same result can be achieved, but on a broader base, by occasionally enclosing, possibly with your statement, a quality check form to your clients asking them to rate you on the different aspects of quality about which you are concerned, in a short checkoff format with opportunity for comment. Ask them to return it with their next correspondence with you so there is no deadline and no inconvenience on their part. This should not take on the appearance of a major general questionnaire, but more of an occasional "how are we doing?" survey. You may get some useful feedback. You may get some complaints. You will certainly project to the client that you are very concerned about quality.

Other less proactive ways that you can assess quality include the price that you are able to charge for the product (it is true that you get what you pay for). The monthly number of cancelled requests will provide an ongoing statistical measurement of quality, especially of response time and availability of resources. The amount of repeat business you receive from a client is indicative of their perception of your business, and a drop off in business probably indicates a problem and time for a phone call. Referrals from other clients is a very positive indication of your quality.

Summary

In order to control quality, we have first defined it by identifying specific characteristics of a product which relate to quality. By looking at each attribute and summarizing the things that could go wrong that may detract from quality, we discovered a list of potential problems that are common to all of the quality characteristics. You may approach quality control by concentrating on a single troublesome aspect and analyzing all of the factors that can affect its contribution to the quality of your product. You may also approach it by looking at all of the potential common sources of problems and in a general approach attempt to preclude a major quality problem by anticipating and creating the most effective working conditions in each of these areas.

Because this is a business, the answer to the question "who cares?" is "your clients," but if you want to control quality, the answer must also be that your staff cares!

Fee-Based Document Delivery: Permissible Activities Under United States Copyright Law

James S. Heller
Director, Law Library
Associate Professor of Law
University of Idaho
Moscow, Idaho

Introduction

The Copyright Act of 1976[1] and interpretative decisional law govern the scope of protection given a copyright owner, as well as the rights of users of copyrighted materials. The rights of a copyright owner include the right to reproduce and distribute copyrighted works, and may, therefore, limit the activities of document delivery services. The Copyright Act does not, however, give the copyright owner a monopoly over subsequent use of copyrighted works. The rights of a copyright owner are subject to other provisions of the Copyright Act that establish rights for users of copyrighted works.[2] This article will discuss permissible activities of fee-based document deliverers, both non-profit and for-profit, under United States copyright law.

Under most circumstances the extent to which a library or information broker may provide copies for a fee will have to be justified under either of two sections of the Copyright Act. Section 107 provides that the fair use of a copyrighted work is not an infringement of copyright. Section 108 of the Act provides that a library may, under certain circumstances, reproduce copyrighted works without subjecting its staff members, the library, or the library's parent organization to liability for copyright infringement. If copying and distribution of copyrighted materials is permitted under the Act, the copyright owner need not be contacted for permission, and royalties need not be paid. Without exemption under the Act, the payment of royalties, or permission to copy by the copyright owner, the reproduction of copyrighted works will likely be considered infringing.

As a general matter a library is liable for infringing acts committed by its employees during the scope of employment, even if the employee had been instructed not to engage in impermissible copying. The parent organization of the library, such as a university or a public library board of trustees, also would be liable for copyright infringement, as would the employee who did the actual copying. As a practical matter, a plaintiff in a copyright infringement suit would seek damages from the institution as well as from the individual. Fee-based document deliverers and their parent organizations should be aware of the rights and limitations of the Copyright Act, and instruct their employees on the limits of permissible copying.

Fair Use — Section 107

Protection under the fair use provision of the Act should be available to both non-profit library document delivery services and to for-profit information brokers. Section 107 states:

"Notwithstanding the provisions of section 106, the fair use of a copyrighted work, including such use by reproduction in copies or phonorecords or by any other means specified by that section, for purposes such as criticism, comment, news reporting, teaching (including multiple copies for classroom use), scholarship, or research, is not an infringement of copyright. In determining whether the use made of a work in any particular case is a fair use the factors to be considered shall include —
(1) the purpose and character of the use, including whether such use is of a commercial nature or is for nonprofit educational purposes;
(2) the nature of the copyrighted work;
(3) the amount and substantiality of the portion used in relation to the copyrighted work as a whole; and
(4) the effect of the use upon the potential market for or value of the copyrighted work."[3]

Section 107 makes no distinction between individual and institutional privileges under the fair use provision. Furthermore, section 108[4] and its legislative history[5] clearly provide that libraries may qualify for protection under section 107. Nevertheless, there is debate concerning the extent to which the fair use provision applies to libraries.

In the 1983 *Report of the Register of Copyrights: Library Reproduction of Copyrighted Works,* the former Register of Copyrights stated that a library's ability to justify copying under section 107 is very limited, and that most library copying must be allowed under section 108, if at all.[6] The Author's League of America and the Association of American Publishers adamantly believe that libraries may reproduce copyright works exclusively under section 108 of the Act.[7]

Notwithstanding the restrictive interpretation of the Register and the authors' and publishers' interest groups, section 107 protection is available to libraries. Generally, if the individual requestor could have made the copy under section 107, the library, acting as the requestor's agent, may legally make the copy.

Section 107 lists four factors that courts must consider in assessing whether a particular use is fair, although factors other than these expressly enumerated may also be considered.[8] The first of those factors is the purpose and character of the use, including whether the use is for a commercial purpose, or, instead, for non-profit educational purposes. While non-profit use may be favored over commercial use, the latter still may be deemed fair.

Although the United States Supreme Court has stated that "[c]opying for commercial gain has a much weaker claim to fair use than copying for personal enrichment,"[9] the fact that a use is for a purpose of financial gain will not necessarily preclude a finding of fair use.[10] Nor, on the other hand, is copying for educational purposes always fair.[11] When a non-profit document deliverer or for-profit information broker copies and distributes copyrighted materials at the request of another party, both the purpose of the copying center in making and distributing the copy and the purpose of the use by the party for whom the copy is made will be considered.

For the non-profit library, the analysis would likely begin with an examination of whether the library charges more for the copy than its reproduction and distribution costs. Those costs may be significant, as they include the cost of acquiring and maintaining equipment, utilities, supplies, postage, and labor. If the library merely recoups its direct and indirect costs of providing a copy and does not "profit" from its document delivery activity, its purpose ought not be considered commercial. Under these circumstances the library's purpose in providing document delivery is to assist in the dissemination of information, which if not considered a non-profit educational purpose, is at the worst benign.

The for-profit information broker is in a significantly different situation. The business of the information broker is to provide documents — either originals or copies — on demand. The company profits by providing the documents, and any copying done pursuant to that end would likely be considered to be for a commercial purpose. Such copying would, in all likelihood, be considered unfair.[12]

Because copies made by non-profit libraries or commercial information brokers are distributed to another party, an examination of how the reproduced material is used by the requesting party is appropriate. There appears to be greater latitude to provide copies for educators, students, or non-profit researchers than there is to make copies for persons in a commercial setting. Still, individuals in a business or corporate setting clearly have some fair use rights to copy materials for the purpose of aiding their understanding. Copying for such a purpose should not presumptively be considered unfair.

The second factor considered in a fair use analysis is the nature of the copyrighted work. As a general matter, copying factual or informational works is more likely to be considered fair than is the copying of creative works.[13] However, recent United States Supreme Court decisions seem to indicate that the nature of the work may be the least important of the four factors.[14]

The third factor considered under section 107 is the amount copied from the copyrighted work. Generally, the more that is copied the less likely it is that the use will be considered fair.[15] Recent Supreme Court decisions, however, indicate more concern with significance rather than quantity of the portion copied.[16] These decisions have focused on the extent to which the copying harmed the copyright owner.

The final fair use factor is the effect of the use upon the potential market for or value of the copyrighted work. In the words of the Supreme Court, this factor has become "undoubtedly the single most important element of fair use."[17] The fair use analysis of the first factor, the purpose of the use, required a consideration of both the purpose of the document deliverer in making the copy and the nature of the use by the party for whom the copy was made. The fourth factor requires a similar two-part analysis.

As the actual copier, the actions of the document deliverer in making and distributing the copy would first be analyzed to determine whether such copying adversely affected the value of the copyrighted work. Second, because the document deliverer acted as the agent of the requestor, an examination as to whether the ultimate use of the copied work harmed the potential market for or value of the copyrighted work would also be appropriate.

The fact that a particular user relies on a document deliverer for a photocopy rather than purchasing the work or paying royalties should not work against a finding of fair use. Making a single copy of an article or excerpt from a book clearly seems to be within the meaning of fair use. Similarly, a document deliverer's copying and distributing a single copy of a copyrighted work upon request would not adversely affect the value of that work. The question of harm to copyright owners becomes more acute, however, when the document deliverer provides copies to users on a large scale, and, perhaps, makes multiple copies of the same material for a variety of different users.

There has been only one decision by an American court that considered the limits of fair use for library document delivery units. In *Williams & Wilkins Co. v. United States*[18] the United States Court of Claims held that large scale copying by the National Library of Medicine was a fair use. The holding has limited precedented value, however,[19] and the scope of fair use for document deliverers remains unsettled.

It is arguable that NLM-type large scale copying by a non-profit library would be permissible under section 107. It is doubtful, however, that such copying by a for-profit information broker would be considered fair use. A consideration of the four fair use factors would likely lead a court to conclude that such copying was infringing. The fact that the for-profit information broker profited from the copying, copied entire articles, and did so on a large scale, would probably result in a finding of copyright infringement. If the commercial document deliverer could not justify the copying under the fair use provision of the Act, the copying would be infringing. Non-profit libraries, however, in addition to being able to justify document delivery under section 107, may also rely on section 108 of the Act.

Copying by Libraries — Section 108

Section 108 of the Copyright Act permits certain copying by libraries or their employees. The express language of section 108 and its legislative history limit protection to libraries, and for-profit information brokers may not claim protection under this section. Commercial information brokers must justify their reproduction and distribution activities under the fair use provision of the Act, if at all.

The Act mandates that copying under section 108 must be done without a purpose of direct or indirect commercial advantage.[20] The legislative history to this section states that the "advantage" referred to must attach to the copying itself.[21] A library that profits from its document delivery activities by charging more than the cost of making and distributing copies may not justify that copying under section 108. Section 108 also requires that the collection of a qualifying library be open to the public or to persons doing research in a specialized field.[22]

The former Register of Copyrights believes that the "commercial advantage" and "open collection" provisions of section 108 limit the ability of libraries in for-profit institutions to qualify for protection under this section.[23] On the contrary, these provisions do not disqualify such libraries from section 108 protection.[24] Still, rarely do libraries in for-profit organizations such as corporations engage in fee-based document delivery activities to persons outside the parent institution.

The question naturally arises whether document delivery units of public or private non-profit institutions, such as public or academic libraries, may claim protection under section 108 as well as under section 107. If the library's collection is open to the public or to researchers, if neither the library nor its document delivery unit reaps direct or indirect commercial gain from the copying, and if the requisite notice of copyright[25] is included with the copy, then section 108 protection should be available.

A library that qualifies for section 108 protection may make a single copy of an article or small excerpt from a copyrighted work if 1) the copy becomes the property of the user; 2) the library had no notice that the copy would be used for a purpose other than private study, scholarship or research; and 3) the library displays warning signs as specified by the Register of Copyrights.[26] It is appropriate, therefore, to consider each of these requirements in determining whether the fee-based document deliverer may provide copies under section 108(d).

Requests for multiple copies may not be provided under section 108(d). In nearly all circumstances when a fee is involved, however, the library will be asked to provide only a single copy of an article or excerpt. The library should also notify requestors that copies provided to them under section 108(d) become their property.

The requirement that the library have no notice that the requested copy will be used for a purpose other than private study, scholarship, or research merits greater analysis. According to the former Register of Copyrights, a library may not reproduce articles or small excerpts for for-profit information brokers under section 108.[27] Furthermore, the Register questioned the legitimacy of copying for job-related purposes under this section.[28] Even if one accepts for argument's sake this restrictive view of permissible copying under section 108, a library providing copies to non-institutional clients for a fee rarely will know that the requestor will use the copy for a purpose other than private study, scholarship, or research.

A library is not prevented from supplying photocopies under section 108 unless it knows of the intended invalid use prior to its copying and distributing the materials. The Register indicates that notice of improper use of the copied materials "could be found in a variety of facts and circumstances."[29] The Register seemingly imposes on a library a duty to discern whether use of the material is for either study, scholarship, or research. Other commentators, on the other hand, place no affirmative burden on the library to predetermine the requestor's intended use of the materials.[30] The Register's standards appear to be too rigorous, as they place an almost impossible burden on libraries. Actual rather than implied knowledge of improper use should be the standard for assessing compliance with this statutory provision.

In a similar vein, one may ask whether after supplying a copy a document deliverer is responsible for subsequent infringing acts by the requestor. Copies provided under section 108 become the property of the requestor. Assuming the library had no notice of an impermissible use by the requestor, it could not be held liable for infringement after the copy was provided. Similarly, copies provided by a document deliverer under section 107 also become the requestor's property, and the document deliverer should incur no liability for subsequent infringing acts.

A library's copying and distribution rights under section 108 are subject to the limitations of subsection (g) of that section. Section 108(g)(1) prohibits related or concerted reproduction of multiple copies of the same material, on one occasion or over a period of time, and either for aggregate use by one or more individuals or for separate use by individual members of a group. However, a library may repeatedly make single copies of the same material on separate occasions to independent users who are not members of a group. In practice, the subsection (g)(1) prohibition against related or concerted reproduction of *multiple* copies would rarely apply to activities of library document deliverers. The purpose of Section 108(g)(1) is to prevent multiple copying of the same materials for persons in a single organization, and fee-based document deliverers generally are not asked to provide this service.

Section 108(g)(2) prohibits the systematic reproduction or distribution of single or multiple copies of the materials described in subsection (d), namely, articles and short excerpts. The subsection (g)(2) limitation addresses single as well as multiple copying, and is probably more applicable to document deliverers than is subsection (g)(1). The apparent purpose of subsection (g)(2) is to prevent copying in such quantities as to reduce the market for a work, whether that market be a subscription to a journal, a single issue of a journal, or even a specific article from a journal. This provision prevents a library from providing copies in such quantities that the requestor receives a substantial portion of a journal without either subscribing to the journal, purchasing an issue, or paying royalties. The fee paid to the library by the requestor cannot be considered a substitute for royalty payments or subscription fees due the copyright owner or publisher. The library's fee is compensation for its labor in providing the copy; none of that fee accrues to the benefit of the copyright owner or publisher.

Over a period of time a fee-based document deliverer may be asked to provide a single user several different articles from the same journal, thus possibly reducing the market for the journal. While the *Guidelines for the Proviso of Subsection (g)(2)* (CONTU Guidelines)[31] obligate requestors to maintain borrowing records,[32] they do not require the lending library to maintain similar records. Consequently, it may be difficult for the document deliverer to determine the point at which it engages in systematic reproduction. The Register of Copyrights has stated that large scale library photocopying services that employ full time staff, advertise, and have "considerably substantial output" may be engaging in systematic copying.[33] Furthermore, the Register believes that libraries utilizing telefacsimile devices to transmit copies possibly operate on such a large scale as to be considered systematic.[34]

The Williams & Wilkins decision, discussed earlier, was decided under the 1909 Copyright Act rather than under the 1976 Act which governs the scope of copyright protection today. Commentators differ regarding how Williams & Wilkins might be decided under the current Act. The Register believes that such copying clearly would not be permitted under the 1976 Act, and that section 108(g)(2) of the Act "reflected a judgment that the copying there [NIH/NLM] was 'systematic' and thus Congress was attempting to render it infringing."[35] In contrast, probably the most noted expert on copyright law, the late Professor Melville Nimmer, believed that NLM's activities were "largely within the permissible area of photocopying under Section 108."[36]

The scope of permissible document delivery activity by libraries under section 108 remains unsettled. The Register's statement that copying by large scale library document delivery units violates the systematic copying prohibition of subsection (g)(2) is overly restrictive. Unfortunately, few if any objective standards exist by which a library may determine whether its document delivery activities are permitted under section 108.

CONTU Guidelines

Guidelines for the Proviso of Subsection 108(g)(2) (CONTU Guidelines) were included in the Conference Report[37] to the copyright revision bill and are part of the legislative history of the Act. Although courts may take judicial notice of the guidelines in determining the scope of activity permitted under section 108(g)(2), the Guidelines are not law. Unfortunately, the Guidelines focus on actions by requesting rather than supplying libraries, and offer little guidance in determining whether a fee-based library document deliverer has engaged in the "systematic reproduction or distribution" prohibited under section 108(g)(2).

CONTU Guideline number three may have some application to libraries providing fee-based document delivery services. That guideline states that interlibrary requests for photocopies should be accompanied by a representation that the request complies with a provision of the Copyright Act or with the Guidelines. Traditionally the requesting library would indicate such compliance on an interlibrary loan form. With the recent popularity of transmitting requests for photocopies electronically, libraries may inadvertently neglect to make the requisite representation. If a request for a photocopy does not include such a representation, the question may reasonably be asked whether that request should be honored.

While the Act itself does not prohibit a library from filling the request, it would be prudent to comply with the Guideline. The document deliverer may ask the requesting library to assert that the request complies with the Guidelines or another provision of the Copyright Act. Alternatively the document deliverer may choose not to fill the request, with an explanation as to why the material was not supplied.

The document deliverer, as the copier of the copyrighted document, may be liable for infringement if the copying is not permitted under either section 107 or section 108 of the Act. Without the requesting library's representation of compliance with the Act or the Guidelines, royalties may be due the copyright owner, and permission to copy may be required. Acting on an incomplete interlibrary loan form clearly puts the burden on the copying institution to comply with the Copyright Act.

Contractual Limitations

An institution may contract away its statutory rights to reproduce and distribute copyrighted works. The Copyright Act provides that section 108 rights do not affect contractual obligations assumed by a library when it obtains a work.[38] Contractual provisions against duplicating books, journals, or information from a data base may limit or bar reproduction under section 108. Similarly, a library may contract away its fair use rights under section 107 of the Act. A library or its document delivery unit should carefully review any contractual provisions affecting its right to reproduce and distribute copyrighted works under the Act prior to agreeing to purchase or lease such materials.

Copyright Clearance Center

Established in late 1977, the Copyright Clearance Center (CCC)[39] operates a centralized photocopy permissions and payment system on behalf of copyright owners, generally publishers. Rather than requesting permission for each act of copying not permitted under the Act, institutional users (called "service users" by the CCC) registered with the CCC pay pre-set royalty fees directly to the Center. After deducting administrative costs, the CCC distributes those royalties to the publishers. As of March 1987, approximately 1,100 publishers were registered with the Center, as were 2,300 service users, including academic and governmental libraries and fee-based information brokers.

The Copyright Clearance Center acknowledges that service users retain their statutory rights under sections 107 and 108 of the Copyright Act.[40] Copying within the CONTU Guidelines also need not be reported.[41] The Copyright Clearance Center does not have monitoring or enforcement capabilities; users report copying they believe requires payment of royalties. If a document deliverer who is a registered CCC service user considers certain copying to be within the scope of section 107 or section 108, it need not report that copying to the Center.

Many of the 55,000 publications registered with the Center contain a publisher drafted permissions policy statement. The statement apprises readers of the publication's registration with the CCC, the copying fee, and the conditions of authorization to copy.[42] Some policy statements directly acknowledge that royalties need not be paid for permissible copying under the Copyright Act. As a general matter, royalties need not be paid for section 107 or 108 copying even without such acknowledgement.

Technically, users do not contract away their statutory rights when they join the CCC, although organizations that purchase photocopy licenses with the Center may agree to waive some of those rights.[43] Unless there is agreement to the contrary, copies legally made do not require the payment of royalties to the CCC. If copying is not permitted under the Act, document deliverers who are registered service users should pay royalties for each copy made.[44]

Document deliverers who are not registered CCC service users pay royalties, if at all, directly to the copyright owner. Document deliverers may, of course, seek permission to copy from the copyright owner in lieu of paying royalties for copying not permitted under the Act. If permission is not granted royalties would be due, although they may differ from the amount established for CCC service users. Merely subscribing to a publication registered with the CCC does not necessarily mean that the document deliverer must pay the royalty fee established by the publisher for CCC service users.

Foreign Works

The major international copyright treaty to which the United States is a party is the Universal Copyright Convention.[45] Members to the Convention agree to provide a level of copyright protection to foreign works at least equal to the protection available to their own citizens.

The United States Copyright Act provides the unpublished works of foreign authors are protected "without regard to the nationality of domicile of the author."[46] Published works are protected under the Act to the same extent as are those of American authors if: at the time the work was first published the author was either domiciled in the United States or was a citizen of a country that is a party to a treaty in which the United States also is a party;[47] the work was first published in the United States or in a foreign nation that on the date of first publication was a party to the Universal Copyright Convention;[48] the work was first published by the United Nations or any of its agencies, or by the Organization of American States;[49] or the work comes within the scope of a Presidential proclamation.[50]

The Universal Copyright Convention requires similar formalities for copyright notice as exist under our Copyright Act, including the copyright owner's name and the year of initial publication.[51] While most photocopying by document deliverers is of works published in the United States, such organizations should be aware that foreign works also may be protected against unauthorized reproduction.

Conclusion

Although document delivery by both commercial and non-profit organizations has become commonplace, the scope of permissible activities by document deliverers under the Copyright Act has yet to be resolved. For-profit information brokers generally may copy and distribute copyrighted materials only under the fair use provision of the Act. If such activity is not permitted under section 107, it would likely be considered infringing without permission of the copyright owner or payment of royalties. Although a library's ability to copy under fair use has been questioned, the Act clearly contemplates reproduction and distribution activities by libraries under both section 107 and section 108. Just as copyright owners do not have a monopoly over subsequent reproduction and distribution of their works, document deliverers must realize that their right to copy and distribute copyrighted works is not unlimited. Document deliverers should be aware of the rights and limitations provided under United States copyright law, and conduct their operations in accordance with the law.

Notes

[1] 17 U.S.C. Secs. 101–801 (1982).

[2] 17 U.S.C. Secs. 107–118 (1982).

[3] 17 U.S.C. Sec. 107 (1982).

[4] "Nothing in this section . . . in any way affects the right of fair use as provided by section 107. . . . " 17 U.S.C. Sec. 108(f)(4) (1982).

[5] H.R. Rep. No. 1476, 94th Cong., 2d Sess. 78–79 (1976) (hereinafter cited as *House Report*).

[6] U.S. Copyright Office, *Report of the Register of Copyrights: Library Reproduction of Copyrighted Works (17 U.S.C. Sec. 108)* Washington, D.C.: U.S. Copyright Office, Library of Congress, 1983), p.95–104 (hereinafter cited as *Register's Report*).

[7] Association of American Publishers and the Authors League of America, *Photocopying by Academic, Public, and Non-profit Research Libraries* (1978), p.3–4,16.

[8] Section 107 states " . . . the facts to be considered shall include. . . . " See also Harper & Row, Inc. v. Nation Enterprises, 471 U.S. 539, 560 (1985).

[9] Sony Corp. of America v. Universal City Studios, 464 U.S. 417, 455 n.40, *reh'g. denied* 465 U.S. 1112 (1984).

[10] Triangle Publications, Inc. v. Knight-Ridder Newspapers, Inc., 626 F.2d 1171, 1175–76 (5th Cir. 1980); Rosemont Enterprise v. Random House, Inc., 366 F.2d 303, 307–08 (2d Cir. 1966), *cert.denied* 385 U.S. 1009 (1967).

[11] Marcus v. Rowley, 695 F.2d 1171, 1175 (9th Cir. 1983); Encyclopedia Britannica Educational Corp. v. Crooks, 542 F.Supp 1156, 1174–1175 (W.D.N.Y. 1982).

[12] The United States Supreme Court has stated that "[e]very commercial use of copyrighted material is presumptively an unfair exploitation of the monopoly privilege that belongs to the owner of the copyright." Sony Corp. of America v. Universal City Studios, 464 U.S. 415, 451, *reh'g. denied* 465 U.S. 1112 (1984), *quoted in* Harper & Row, Publishers, Inc. v. Nation Enterprises, 471 U.S. 539, 562 (1985). In the Nation decision the Court also stated that "[t]he crux of the profit/nonprofit motive distinction is not whether the sole motive of the use is monetary gain but whether the user stands to profit from exploitation of the copyrighted material without paying the customary price." 471 U.S. at 562 (1985).

[13] Harper & Row, Publishers, Inc., v. Nation Enterprises, 471 U.S. 539, 563 (1985).

[14] *See* Sony Corp. of America v. Universal City Studies, Inc. 464 U.S. 417, *reh'g. denied* 465 U.S. 1112 (1984); Harper & Row, Publishers, Inc. v. Nation Enterprises, 471 U.S. 539 (1985). The Nation court focused on the fact that the copied work was as yet unpublished in discussing the "nature of the work copied.". 471 U.S. at 564.

[15] Walt Disney Productions v. Air Pirates, 581 F.2d 751, 757–58 (9th Cir. 1978), *cert. denied* 439 U.S. 1132 (1979); Whitol v. Crow, 309 F.2d 777 (8th Cir. 1962).

[16] Sony Corp. of America v. Universal City Studies, Inc., 464 U.S. 417, 449–50, *reh'g. denied* 465 U.S. 1112 (1984); Harper & Row, Publishers, Inc. v. Nation Enterprises, 471 U.S. 539, 564–66 (1985).

[17] Harper & Row, Publishers, Inc. v. Nation Enterprises, 471 U.S. 539, 566 (1985).

[18] 487 F.2d 1345 (Ct. Cl. 1973), *aff'd. by an equally divided court*, 420 U.S. 376 (1975).

[19] The Williams & Wilkins decision was affirmed by the United States Supreme Court in a four-to-four decision. Such decisions, while binding on the parties, are not dispositive of the issue in subsequent cases. Trans World Airlines, Inc. v. Hardison, 432 U.S. 63, 73 (1977).

[20] 17 U.S.C. Sec. 108(a)(1) (1982).

[21]House Report, *supra* note 5, at 75.

[22]17 U.S.C. Sec. 108(a)(2) (1982).

[23]Register's Report, *supra* note 6, at 75–79. The Register stated that in for-profit institutions "the collection must be 'open to the employees of its competitors.' " *Id.* at 78.

[24]As to the commercial advantage provision, see House Report, *supra* note 5, at 75. Regarding open collections, some commentators believe that this requirement may be satisfied by access to a library's collection either by personal visits or through interlibrary loan. James Heller & Sarah Wiant, *Copyright Handbook* (Littleton, Colo.: Rothman [for Amer. Assoc. of Law Libraries], 1984), p. 16.

[25]17 U.S.C. Sec. 108(a)(3) (1982).

[26]17 U.S.C. Sec. 108(d) (1982). The language of the warning sign may be found at 37 C.F.R. 201.14 (1986).

[27]Register's Report, *supra* note 6, at 120.

[28]*Id.* at 225.

[29]*Id.* at 121.

[30]James Treece, Library Photocopying, *UCLA Law Review* 24:1025, 1050 (1977).

[31]H.R. Conf. Rep. No. 1733, 94th Cong. 2d Sess. 72–73 (1976).

[32]Guideline number four, *Id.* at 73.

[33]Register's Report, *supra* note 6, at 140.

[34]*Id.* at 262.

[35]*Id.* at 130.

[36]Melville Nimmer, *Nimmer on Copyright* (New York, N.Y.: Matthew Bender, 1986), Vol. 3, Sec. 13.05 [E][4][d].

[37]H.R. Conf. Rep. No. 1733, 94th Cong. 2d Sess. 72–73 (1976).

[38]17 U.S.C. Sec. 108(f)(4) (1982).

[39]21 Congress Street; Salem, MA 01970; (617) 744-3350.

[40]Copyright Clearance Center, Inc., *Handbook for Libraries and Other Organizational Users which Copy From Serials and Separates: Procedures for Using the Programs of the Copyright Clearance Center, Inc.* (Salem, Mass.: October 1977) p. 6, 10. A brochure currently distributed by the CCC states: "The copyright law makes provisions for no-fee copying under limited 'fair use' conditions described in Section 107. Certain libraries are granted additional no-fee copying rights under . . . Section 108. However, frequent needs for copying copyrighted works, when permission is necessary, arise *outside* the infringement-exempt conditions of Sections 107 and 108." Copyright Clearance Center, Inc., *Now You Can Photocopy and Still Comply With the Copyright Law.*

[41]The former program director of the Association of American Publishers Copyright Clearance Center Task Force, who was also vice-president, secretary, and director of the CCC, stated in 1977: "[t]he participation of a library will be determined by whether or not that library has requirements for its own purposes that exceed the CONTU Guidelines or fair use. In other words, if they don't, they won't have to report anything because the program is predicated on a method of permitting the making of copies when you need them and when your need exceeds CONTU guidelines and fair use." Ben Weil, "Copying Access Mechanisms," *IEEE Transactions on Professional Communications*, PC–20: 173 (1977).

[42]Copyright Clearance Center, Inc., *PPC (Publisher's Photocopy Fee Catalog)* (Salem, Mass.: July 1986) Introduction.

[43]As of March 1987, twenty-two corporations had purchased annual photocopy licenses with the Copyright Clearance Center. Under the licensing agreement, the corporation pays an annual fee to the CCC, based on a sixty day sampling of its copying, in lieu of periodic reporting. Publishers determine the royalty fee, and many waive a certain percentage of the fee as a fair use allowance.

[44]If the *requesting* institution is a registered CCC service user, and if the article requested to be copied has the CCC notice, royalties need not be paid if the copying is permitted under the Copyright Act.

[45]The United States is not a party to the Berne Convention, to which most major nations have acceded.

[46]17 U.S.C. Sec. 104(a) (1982).

[47]17 U.S.C. Sec. 104(b)(1) (1982). The United States is a party to the Mexico City Convention and the Buenos Aires Convention as well as to the UCC.

[48]17 U.S.C. Sec. 104(b)(2) (1982).

[49]17 U.S.C. Sec. 104(b)(3) (1982).

[50]17 U.S.C. Sec. 104(b)(4) (1982).

[51]The Buenos Aires Convention requires the notice "All Rights Reserved."

Policy:
Help or Hurdle?

Miriam A. Drake
Director of Libraries
Georgia Institute of Technology
Atlanta, Georgia

Introduction

When I was invited to speak at this conference, I was asked to address four questions;

1. Should any academic library start a fee-based service for business?

2. How does a fee-based service affect fund raising efforts, if at all?

3. What are the pros and cons of having a fee-based service as a separate service and as part of another service? and

4. What is a good mix of the level of staff needed to make such a venture work well?

I will answer those questions and discuss other aspects of fee-based services which are critical to the success of the operation.

Role of Policy

Before delving into the meat of the issues we need to look at process and context. First, why do we have policies? What do they do for us? Do they get in the way, or can they facilitate what we want to do?

In a well run organization, policies play an important and positive role. They are not ends in themselves but tools to help the organization achieve its objectives and purposes. Policies should be enabling statements rather than obstacle courses, and should be an integral part of that long and often difficult process of planning and choosing.

Ideally, an organization initially decides why it exists. What are its purposes or missions? It then decides on what it wants to achieve in terms of specific achievements. The next step is to formulate policies to provide a framework for day-to-day decisions and a mechanism to achieve objectives and realize the goals of the organization. In the real world, however, things seldom happen that way. Most libraries do not have viable mission statements, goals, or a clear vision of why they exist and what they want to accomplish. Typically, library policies are formulated in a vacuum and address symptoms rather than operational issues. They often are framed as a response to a crisis or an exceptional situation rather than the norm.

Most universities have mission statements which state that the purpose of the institution is to provide instruction, research, and service. Few have translated those terms into operational goals and objectives. What do those words, "instruction," "research," and "service" mean? What role do they dictate for the library? The answer to that question relates to the first question I mentioned: Should any academic library start a fee-based service for business? My answer to this question is a resounding *no*.

Legal Considerations

While the word "service" appears in the mission statements of most large universities in this country, it does not imply service to industry and business. In small universities or colleges the term "service" may mean keeping "town and gown" relationships positive by offering entertainment, courses, football tickets, and other amenities to the local community or state politicians. In land grant universities, service usually means the agricultural extension service and possibly an industrial extension service. It may or may not be an enabling framework for fee-based information services.

Some states are becoming increasingly hostile to not-for-profit organizations of any kind competing with private business. For example, in 1981, the Arizona legislature passed a bill which states "colleges and universities may not sell goods or services that are available from private enterprises unless those goods or services are an integral part of research or instruction." In 1985, Louisiana enacted legislation that requires the Board of Regents "to adopt a grievance procedure for business owners who think they have been hurt by 'unreasonable competition' from colleges and universities." Pennsylvania's legislation is in the planning stage and it will require "non-profit organizations to allocate all the profits from profit-making ventures to the 'primary purpose' of the organization and to report to the state on all revenue sources."[1]

Complaints about unfair competition from small businesses prompted a General Accounting Office investigation into the business activities of universities and other not-for-profit organizations. Small business owners alleged that not-for-profit organizations had too much of a competitive advantage in the sales of goods and services and urged Congress to restrict these activities or levy new taxes on these operations. While the GAO concluded that there was not sufficient evidence to support the claims, it said, " . . . that the issue will draw increased attention in the next few years."[2]

The 1986 tax law is far stricter on "unrelated business income" and taxes on that income than the previous tax code. The new law imposes more stringent requirements on 501(c)(3) organizations.

If the university defines services to business and industry in its mission statement, then fee-based library and information services might be considered part of its usual business. Under some of these statutes private business could bring action against a university providing fee-based information services. Ultimately, these issues will be decided in the courts but will depend on the state law, interpretation of the tax code, the mood of the judge, and how well the university has defined its mission.

Staff and Administration Attitudes

Usually, the biggest obstacle to fee-based services comes from the library staff, university administration, or faculty. Most library staff were educated in an era when the library was a warehouse to which they should provide access. Their job was to teach people how to find information for themselves in card catalogs, printed indexes, books, and journals. When abstracting and indexing services went online and libraries began using OCLC, RLIN or others for cataloging, the role changed to providing access to online citation data bases and documents. Meanwhile, people were beginning to have an appreciation for the value of time. The heart of the university is not the library, it is the faculty member's time and creative energies. When libraries established fees for online searching, many libraries took an apologetic attitude. "We had no choice." "Our budget does not provide for online searching." "We would rather provide online searching at no cost, but what can we do?" Despite rapid changes in technology and changing attitudes on the part of our users and clients, many librarians are still in the rut of paper and have no concept of value added services. They believe their job is finished when they deliver a document or print-out of citations.

Ron Dubberly offered four alternatives to charging fees in public libraries: increasing revenues at the institutional level, increasing efficiency of existing resources, limiting service, and restructuring service priorities.[3]

Many librarians would agree with Dubberly's proposals. If you can't offer a service at no out-of-pocket cost to the user, don't offer it. While these proposals may sound nice to the "do gooders," they are not practical and do not serve the needs of the people whom we serve. All libraries should be looking toward expanding services which provide value to the consumer, not contracting them.

Access is another apologia for staying in the rut. The people who use this strategy have failed to see that access is not the issue, usage is the issue. Someone once described a library as "thought in cold storage." It is likely to remain that way unless we, the librarians, begin to offer services that provide value and quality for the consumer. The traditional forms of "access" are outrageously expensive for the consumer in terms of the value of time. If we look at the average salaries of management and engineering faculty, attorneys, business people, and others, it quickly becomes apparent that librarians can offer cost effective and valuable services. This is not a result of our lower salaries. It is a result of our knowledge of how to find information and produce it more efficiently and effectively than an individual faced with a stack of books, journals, A & I volumes, or print-outs. Librarians have the opportunity of a lifetime to demonstrate their value as opposed to the value of their collections. Information in books and data bases is just information in containers. It requires the skills of information professionals to extract, evaluate, and synthesize it into a useful product.

Faculty in the university may object to fee-based services on two grounds. First, they fear that materials may be outside the library when they need them. Second, they fear that people who pay will get better services than they do. In some institutions, they are probably right. Libraries not paying attention to faculty services and providing different sets of services for paying and non-paying customers will run into this objection. Faculty forced to come to the library to sign out a book or look for information on their own may resent the idea that information rather than access is delivered to the paying customer.

University administrators may take a positive, neutral, or negative position or simply decree that fee-based services won't be allowed. These attitudes stem from their ignorance of the value of information and their failure to see the library organization as an asset with marketable value.

We should be equally wary of the overly enthusiastic administrator who believes that the fees collected will fund the entire library budget and bring in millions in contributions as well. An administrator viewing a business plan projecting several hundred thousand dollars in sales may fail to look at the expense side and unrealistically assume that the income will pay for books and journals as well as staff salaries. The administrator also may view a marketing plan unrealistically and conclude that if corporations are willing to pay fifty or one hundred dollars an hour for information services, surely they will contribute thousands to the institution. These administrators fail to realize that the corporate information consumers usually are not the same people who decide on corporate contributions.

Internal Staffing

⌈Many libraries do not have appropriate staff to operate a fee-based service. People who work in a fee-based operation need to understand the concept of value. Their focal point should be value to the customer, not the library and not documents and books⌋

⌈Staff in fee-based operations need to have a fundamental understanding of how business works. It is not academe⌋ Values and time tables are different. Decisions are not necessarily made the way they are in academe. If that were the case our economy would be in worse shape than it is now.

Staff have to understand marketing as well as markets. They need to have an understanding of costs and pricing. They have to understand the differences between selling, marketing, and public relations. In short, they have to realize that they are in business. Before setting policies about pricing they need to fully understand costs and how they work on the campus. Each campus treats indirect costs differently, and it is essential to understand the accounting system. ⌈They need to know their pricing objectives. Are prices cost-based or value-of-service based? Should prices recover all costs? Direct costs? Indirect costs? Produce a profit? Can we define profit within the context of the university accounting system?⌋

What are the pros and cons of having a fee-based service as a separate service and as part of another service? My answer to that depends on the experience of staff with business and industry and the goals of the operation. If public service or ILL staff demonstrate a demand from business for the service, understand the principles of running a business, and understand the goals of their business, then fee-based service could be integrated into an existing operation. If the talents and attitudes for running a fee-based service successfully are not present in the library, then running it as a separate operation might be more successful. Existing staff may resent having to keep track of their time and out-of-pocket costs. They may feel that their job is to serve students and faculty, not outsiders. They often don't realize the value of their own time or the time of others.

A separate service has the advantages of being easier to administer. It has the drawbacks of staff jealousies, imagined privileges, and resentment. Machiavelli said, "The initiator has the enmity of all who would profit by the preservation of the *old* institutions." Preservation of the old ways is very important to many of our colleagues. When a separate fee-based service is instituted, staff members in other areas may perceive the new staff as a threat. They may feel that fee-based staff are treated better because they bring in money and can show a bottom line for their work. They may imagine that fee-based staff can somehow circumvent the rules for the benefit of their clients. They may feel that fee-based staff have more fun because they are part of the larger community. In my own institution the combination of fee-based services to industry, ILL, and on-campus delivery services operates well. The staff understand that all library clients and users are important. I am not sure it would work as well in other institutions.

Level and Mix of Staffing

There is no magic formula to the level and mix of staffing. It depends on whether it is a separate or integrated operation. If it is a separate organization, greater amounts of staffing will be needed than if it is an integrated operation. In a separate operation there is no opportunity to cross-train staff and use idle time. In an integrated operation there probably will be more hands to do the work and more talent available.

Before considering the question of fund raising, several other important issues need to be addressed, including copyright law, downloading, and the handling of sensitive information.

Copyright

As Mr. Heller said in his paper, the jury is still out on copyrights, and decisions are likely to become increasingly complex as print reproduction technology changes. Publishers are becoming increasingly protective of their property and rights. A number of campuses are investigating operation of data bases on their own computers. Georgia Tech has implemented such a program. Each data base publisher has a different set of rules. Some say that the system can be made available only to students and faculty. Others say it can be used by anyone who walks in the door. Others will say that it cannot be used in an information brokerage operation without royalties. Others want the library to pay royalties on the basis of hits regardless of users.

Downloading

Another area requiring great care is downloading. Each vendor has different rules. In academic settings there is a tendency to share resources and searches through downloading. While these practices save money, they may violate the law and are unethical. Many data base producers will allow downloading for classroom use but it is best to have an agreement on such matters. Downloading from data bases running on Georgia Tech's computers is forbidden except for faculty maintaining personal bibliographies. Our staff have been told that they cannot run searches for other libraries with these data bases.

CD-ROM producers are grappling with the same complications. Some write clauses into their contracts specifying that libraries cannot resell the service. Yet, the service may be a great tool for serving needs of fee paying clients. If prices are structured to recover all costs of providing the service, then prices need to reflect the cost of obtaining resources, such as data bases on CD-ROM. The technology is way ahead of the law, and at present the only way we can deal with this situation is on a case by case basis. What is the copyright status of a document that was put together from several sources? The value added portion of our services stems, in part from repackaging information and customizing the data. How does "fair use" apply to online data and CD-ROM products? Many publishers fail to see that pulling a document off a data base is not fundamentally different from photocopying a document from a book, except in the case of numeric data. In this instance, the online data base or CD-ROM offers significant added value. Obtaining data in machine readable form saves the cost of keying for the user.

On the other side, many librarians fail to see that many online data bases and CD-ROM are fundamentally different from books and journals because the producer has added value to the raw product. The computer gives an advantage to the publisher or producer because of record keeping capabilities. We had no record keeping capabilities with printed works. Unless we did a special study, we could not tell a publisher how many times a document or statistical compilation had been used.

Sensitive Information

Another problem is the government's attempts to restrict the distribution of unclassified but sensitive information and the government's attempts to find out who is using what. The service products and information packages we provide for industry and business must be proprietary and shared with no one. Many states have laws protecting records of library use; however, these laws can be circumvented by use of a court order or subpoena. While the infamous Poindexter memo has been rescinded by the White House, NSDD No. 145 remains. This directive gives the Pentagon the authority to withhold sensitive information and provides the means for DOD or NSC to determine what is or is not made available on private sector data bases. This directive is in total opposition to the President's desires, expressed in another directive, to disseminate scientific and technical information to improve our position in the world economy.

Fund Raising

Fee-based services can be the stimulus for increased contributions from corporations. It requires a very close working relationship between the Library and the Development group. It requires that the Library emphasize customers' satisfaction. If customers are not satisfied, they will not give. This collaboration requires that Development Staff understand that information is a valuable asset to industry and is a competitive tool, a commodity with economic value. The Library often is the first contact a company has with the University. If that contact is successful, it will lead not only to repeat business but also to corporate interest in other programs. At Georgia Tech, we work closely with the Development Staff and the Corporate Liaison Program. We are fortunate because from its earliest days Georgia Tech has had close ties to business and industry.

Conclusion

In summary, fee-based services are appropriate for universities which have created the context for their existence. Policy should nourish these services, not hamper them. We should not create these services in a hostile environment.

Benjamin Disraeli observed, "Men are not the creatures of circumstances. Circumstances are the creatures of men." In order to make fee-based services work successfully, we have to create the appropriate circumstances. In more traditional institutions the creation process will be long and hard. In others, it will be quick and easy. The creation of a fee-based service is one thing; successful operation and repeat business are another. Successful operation requires an environment favorable to fee-based services, an understanding of the nuts and bolts of business, markets, marketing, selling, and public relations.

I will leave you with a story from the advertising business. Before the mass production of MBA's, when I was in the advertising business, we used to spend a lot of time discussing the differences between selling, marketing, and public relations. A story I used was based on my relationships with men. If a man told me how great he was and what he could do for me, he was selling. If he asked me about my dreams, hopes, ambitions and needs, he was marketing. If my best friend told me how great he was, that was public relations. Thank you very much.

Notes

[1] *The Chronicle of Higher Education*, February 11, 1987, p. 22.

[2] American Council on Education, *Higher Education and National Affairs*, 36, April 6, 1987, p. 6.

[3] Dubberly, Ronald A., Managing Not to Charge Fees, *American Libraries*, 17, October 1986, p. 670.

Small Group Discussions

Compiled and edited by Debra R. Schneider
and Anne K. Beaubien
The University of Michigan
Ann Arbor, Michigan

During the conference there was one planned opportunity for small group discussions. The conference organizers prepared a list of questions centered on the area of ethics in fee-based services. Small groups were invited to discuss these questions or bring up and talk about areas of individual interest. The highlights of these discussions are summarized below.

Organizational and Staff Issues

Defining "cost recovery" was of primary interest to several groups. One group surveyed its members and found that the definition varied. One member recovers costs of student workers and supplies; another must recover all those costs plus all salaries, fringe benefits, equipment, space, and overhead. Someone suggested that seed money was essential, and that it usually takes three to five years to recover costs.

Costs might include: reshelving, utilities, space, supplies, salaries (including a fee paid for administration, personnel, and other staff who perform some functions for the service), benefits, marketing, advertising, serials subscriptions, other reference material usage, equipment purchase and repair, collection use, preservation wear and tear, the costs of collecting materials with the library's budget for fee clients, OCLC/RLIN usage, electronic mail, telecommunications, university support, and personnel support.

Relationships between regular and fee-based services staff were also of interest. Group members suggested that fee-based workers may have enhanced images, more self-esteem, and be offered opportunities to earn extra money by free-lancing searches after hours. This could affect internal relations. Fee-based workers should take care to create and maintain good relationships with all staff. Those with authority should engineer circumstances so that all librarians on the staff are congratulated for being far-sighted in having such a service in the library. Reference librarians might be paid for doing off-hour searches.

Fee-based service staff must also "court" other local librarians. Good relations with both on- and off-campus librarians can provide fee-based services with additional resource people and a good source for client referrals.

61

The question of book loans was addressed, and the concensus was that loans were generally not a problem. Different services have a variety of policies on book loans ranging from no loans to extensive loan privileges. There was discussion of whether fee-based services should impact the collection. One institution would like to use non-primary clientele requests to help decide on future purchases; others thought this was an interesting idea but might not be feasible in their institutions.

The question: "Should the librarian and other employees of a fee-based service have a different salary scale than other employees?" generated two different responses. The first was to pay all staff members the same — it's not worth the animosity that could be caused by two pay scales. The idea of bonuses was brought up, and some thought that fee-based service staffers could be offered additional benefits instead. The second response was to pay fee-based staffers more because more risks are involved and extensive sales work is required to be successful. The group did recognize the difficulties involved in creating a two-tiered pay scale. They also suggested additional benefits such as paid conference attendance as substitute payoffs.

All groups agreed that fee-based service success lies in serving the needs of the business community well. Corporate needs are best met by learning and fulfilling their expectations for quality. It was remarked that fee-based services should not be a one-person service that shuts down when that one person is gone. Billing should be done promptly; clients should not be required to be present during a database search; and clients should be informed when there are delays. The fee-based service must make it easy for clients to get the information they need.

Fee/Free

There was a general sense that the fee vs. free question had been well covered in other forums and was of marginal interest to the attendees. Areas that were addressed on this topic were:

While academic freedom in a state-supported institution might be guaranteed by law, providing free access and charging a fee for assistance could be a workable compromise. The general feeling was that creating better access warrants fees.

The fee/free question was thought to be a problem more related to the public or private status of the institution. Concern was expressed about creating an information elite related to the patron's ability to pay. One attendee suggested that fee-based services provide a list of free alternatives to those unable or unwilling to pay.

Malpractice/Liability/Copyright

Verbal and written disclaimers including a record of institution policies on malpractice were considered essential. One group suggested the following:

1. Use disclaimers, both verbal and contractual

2. Let clients derive the search terms to help prevent misunderstood search strategies

3. Use the existing malpractice/liability blanket policy of the institution to cover the fee-based services

4. Establish and maintain a plain-brown-wrapper policy for ensuring client confidentiality

Another group suggested that a malpractice disclaimer could be included in the brochure. This, however, could also give the client the idea to sue. The fee-based service should consult with the institution's legal department for wording of a hold-harmless clause. The clause might also be read to new clients on the phone.

The following "what if" question was addressed by one group:

"A large corporation calls to request the organizational charts of its closest competitors. You call these companies and request their charts, naming yourself only as a representative of the XYZ State University Library. Is this ethical?"

This group thought it would not be ethical to misrepresent themselves when seeking information from one company for another. They would try to get information from a published source such as an annual report. They referred to the Mintz article (see bibliography) for discussions on this issue. Differences between primary and published material were discussed, and a question arose as to whether any guidelines existed on researching these types of problems.

A second question was asked about a fee-based service working for two clients on the same research question (e.g., two sides of a legal case). All agreed that working for both sides when clients request the same information is acceptable as long as confidentiality is not violated. Attendees would charge the same fee to both clients.

Copyright was thoroughly discussed during the regular session on this topic. During group discussions the following were identified as useful:

1. Pay Copyright Clearance Center charges to avoid problems.

2. Keep records to prove copyright compliance.

3. Inform clients of laws by stamping requests or sending handouts.

Quality Issues/Marketing

The following were identified as essentials in building clientele:

1. Create and maintain quality services.

2. Communicate with clients by providing timely status reports on their requests.

3. Make personal contact. The best way to make an impression is by visiting potential clients in person.

4. Create a glossy, quality brochure. Follow up on mailings with personal phone calls.

5. Obtain names of potential clients by buying mailing lists and sending

brochures to the executive branch of targeted corporations. The executive will forward the brochure to the information agent and in this way could become an advocate for the fee-based service.

6. When making phone contacts, smile while talking. It makes a difference.

List of Questions

The questions and topics prepared by conference organizers and presented to the participants to foster discussion are listed below:

General

1. A large local business employs students from a University in which a fee-based service operates. This business had formerly used the service, but upon discovering that students could receive free online searches, had their student employees request searches for them from the regular reference department. Noting a big increase in the number and cost of online searches, the head of reference consulted with the fee-based service head, and it was determined that the business was circumventing the system. What could and should be done in this situation?

2. What are the implications of client confidentiality? Is it important? How far should the fee-based service go in concealing a client's identity?

3. It could be argued that charging fees for a service that used to be provided for free impinges on intellectual freedom. What are the pros and cons of this issue?

4. Are there ways that academic fee-based services can cooperate with one another (or with private brokers) to accomplish their work more effectively? Should there be different library policies for private or academic information brokers?

5. A client calls and requests research on a topic, explaining that he or she is preparing for a lawsuit. The next day, a second client calls asking essentially the same question. You find out that the second client is on the opposing side in the lawsuit.

   a. Is it ethical to work for both at the same time?

   b. Are there legal implications should your service's work become known to both sides?

   c. The research goes much faster the second time due to the similar search strategy. How do you charge for it, knowing that had you not done the same search, it would have taken longer and cost more?

6. A large corporation calls to request the organizational charts of its closest competitors. You call these companies and request their charts, naming yourself only as a representative of the XYZ State University Library. Is this ethical? Why or why not?

7. When creating a fee-structure, what (if any) impact would the following have:

   a. The client is an individual doing personal research.

   b. The client is an alumnus of the university doing personal reserach.

    c. The client is an alumnus and is doing research for his or her company.

    d. The client is a local small business.

    e. The client works for a giant corporation.

    f. The client is another information broker.

8. You are considering starting a fee-based service at your publicly funded university. As you proceed through your planning and information gathering process, a state legislator hears of it and publicly voices his opposition on the grounds that a publicly funded institution should not compete with private businesses. What would you do to convince this individual and others that the service is important, necessary, and a valid use of public funds? If you can't convince him, what do you do next?

Marketing

9. There are several schools of thought on how to market a fee-based service. One suggests that all products and services are successfully marketed using techniques similar to those used in selling commercial items such as cars or stock broker services. Are these techniques appropriate to a service based in an academic library? Why or why not?

10. Your fee-based service provides such excellent service that several of your clients have decided to create in-house libraries and employ their own staff. One or two even ask you to train their new people. What do you do? How do you retain these clients?

Circulation

11. Non-university affiliated information brokers regularly use a library in which a fee-based service exists. They are charged a nominal fee to obtain library cards. Some problems have occurred, particularly with a broker who regularly charges out hundreds of books to re-circulate to clients. There also seems to be an increase in stolen books and articles torn from journals. What are the options in dealing with these problems in both a public and private college setting?

12. Discuss the issue of loaning books to non-university affiliates from an institution whose primary goal is to support the research of the faculty. What could be done if a faculty member should complain about book loans to corporations?

Malpractice

13. What is "information malpractice?" What can be done to 1) prevent it and 2) survive accusations of it?

14. What kinds of contracts should a fee-based service enter into with its clients? How can these protect against malpractice? How can they help/hinder the service provider? The client?

15. In Burlington, Vermont in 1976, Dun & Bradstreet employed a 16-year-old high school student to report on activities in the U.S. Federal Bankruptcy Court. The student mistakenly reported that Greenmoss Builders had filed for bankruptcy. This inaccurate information was published in a credit reporting database. In the subsequent lawsuit, D & B paid out over

$500,000 dollars in awards and damages. This case raises a number of problems for the fee-based provider. These include:

    a. What are the responsibilities (real and implicit) of the fee-based researcher in insuring against providing "dirty data"?

    b. What are the implications of hiring students and other non-professionals to handle such areas as client communications, document delivery, and even "supportive" research?

    c. What role should the librarian play in investigating the accuracy of various online and manual information services? And how is this done within often restrictive time frames and budgets?

    d. What need is there for "information malpractice insurance" — are individuals covered by the institution's policy or are they also personally liable (as is the case in a copyright violation)?

16. An attorney has requested a search on some specific clinical diagnostic techniques to be used in a lawsuit. What can the fee-based researcher do to help insure that the fee-based service will not become a target for a lawsuit should the case be lost?

Copyright

17. A fee-based service is based in the Engineering Sciences Library. This library is not part of the campus-wide library system. The service often receives requests for items not owned by the Engineering Library, but available in one of the system libraries. The fee-based service would like to fill these requests but is concerned by potential copyright problems involved in the photocopying of information not owned by its library. Discuss the pros and cons of copying from other libraries.

18. What are the implications of downloading database searches for permanent storage? What if you download a search for a client, reformat it, print it, and send him the printed version while retaining the disk for "your files"?

19. Should you ask a corporate client what the application of the information would be? Should you document this in case violation of copyright problems arise? What are the costs or other implications of doing the previous?

Organizational Issues

20. Discuss organizational, political, and other issues involved in having the fee-based service report to the following supervisors:

    a. the head of reference

    b. the head of the library in which the service is housed

    c. the Assistant Librarian for Public Services

    d. the director of the library

Give some other suggestions for an organizational structure.

21. Should the librarian and other employees of a fee-based service in an academic library have a different salary scale than other university employees (skills are somewhat different and the fee-based service brings in its own revenue)? What if the service is not breaking even?

Biographies of the Authors

ANNE K. BEAUBIEN
Head, Cooperative Access Services
The University of Michigan Libraries
Ann Arbor, Michigan

Anne K. Beaubien has been head of Cooperative Access Services at the University of Michigan Libraries since 1985. CAS includes MITS (Michigan Information Transfer Source), Interlibrary Loan (borrowing and lending), a faculty microcomputer center, and 747-FAST, a library campus delivery service for faculty which she created in 1986. In 1980 she created MITS and has been its director since that time. From 1971–1980 she was Reference Librarian and Bibliographic Instructor for the social sciences in the Graduate Library at The University of Michigan. She taught in the School of Library Science at The University of Michigan spring terms from 1976–1981. Beaubien has been active in ALA and SLA and is currently on the ALA Association of College and Research Libraries Board of Directors.

Publications include *Learning the Library: Concepts and Methods for Effective Bibliographic Instruction* (Bowker, 1982). Beaubien has spoken widely on information brokering, bibliographic instruction, and database searching. She completed a B.A. in social sciences at Michigan State University in 1969 and an A.M.L.S. at the University of Michigan in 1970. Awards include 1982 Ann Arbor Businesswoman of the Year award and 1987 Distinguished Alumnus Award from the School of Information and Library Studies at The University of Michigan.

TRACY M. CASORSO
INQUIRE
The Gelman Library
George Washington University
Washington, D.C.

Tracy Casorso began her appointment at Gelman Library in 1986, at the time formal planning and preparation for a fee-based service was being initiated. Ms. Casorso has since assumed full responsibility for the implementation, development, and management of Gelman Library's fee-based research and document delivery service called INQUIRE. Operating on a full cost-recovery basis, INQUIRE commenced services in late 1986.

A diverse work history has proven helpful in developing the many skills needed in her current position. Previous library experience includes reference work at both the Kresge Business Administration Library and the Documents Center at Harlan Hatcher Graduate Library of The University of Michigan, and administration of a residence hall library at The University of Michigan. Related work experience includes the day-to-day management of a large apartment complex and experience as a business English instructor in Japan for corporate executives.

Ms. Casorso received her B.S. in business administration from Aquinas College (Grand Rapids, MI) and her A.M.L.S. from The University of Michigan.

MIRIAM A. DRAKE
Director of Libraries
Georgia Institute of Technology
Atlanta, Georgia

Miriam Drake is currently Director of Libraries at the Georgia Institute of Technology. Previous positions include Assistant Director for Library Support Services and Professor of Library Science at Purdue University; private consultant to numerous insurance and accounting firms; Research Associate at the Rockford Research Institute; Marketing Services Assistant and Librarian at Kenyon & Eckhardt, Inc.; and Associate at United Research, Inc. She is a Councilor at Large for the American Library Association and serves on the editorial boards of two professional journals. She has also served on the congressional Office of Technology Assessment's panel on Technology, Public Policy and the Changing Nature of Federal Information Dissemination, and as Chairperson of the OCLC Board of Trustees.

Her publication areas include articles on user fees, information and corporate culture, and the library in the year 2000.

JAMES S. HELLER
Director, Law Library
Associate Professor of Law
University of Idaho College of Law
Moscow, Idaho

James S. Heller is director of the law library and associate professor of law at the University of Idaho College of Law. He formerly served as head of reader services at the George Washington University Law Library, and as director of the Civil Division Library of the United States Department of Justice. He received a B.A. from The University of Michigan, a J.D. Cum Laude from the University of San Diego School of Law, and an M.L.S. from the University of California School of Library and Information Studies. Professor Heller has authored articles on copyright law and, with Sarah K. Wiant, co-authored *Copyright Handbook,* published in 1984 as part of the American Association of Law Libraries' Publication Series. Professor Heller has spoken widely on issues of copyright, particularly as they relate to libraries.

J. MICHAEL HOMAN
Head of Information Services &
Central Technical Documents
Upjohn Company
Kalamazoo, Michigan

J. Michael Homan is in charge of planning, directing, and evaluating the Upjohn Corporate Technical Library's Information Services and Central Technical Documents programs. His responsibilities cover the areas of circulation, reference, current awareness, retrospective searching, user education, online training, and the corporate information systems. He received a B.A. from the University of Chicago's Graduate Library School, and is certified in Medical Librarianship.

Mr. Homan has written and spoken extensively in the areas of health science and pharmaceutical librarianship. He is on the Board of Directors of the Medical Library Association and has been active on the state level in organizations such as the Special Library Association, Michigan Database Users Group (MIDBUG), and the Michigan Health Sciences Library Association.

ELIZABETH LUNDEN
Director of the Learning Resource Center
North Harris County College, East Campus
Houston, Texas

Elizabeth Lunden is currently Director of the Learning Resource Center at North Harris County College. She served as Director of the Regional Information and Communication Exchange (RICE), a fee-based service of Rice University in Houston and held administrative positions in public libraries in Chicago.

Ms. Lunden was co-founder and first chair of the ALA ACRL Discussion Group: Fee-based Service Centers in Academic Libraries (FISCAL). She has written and spoken about fee-based research and was a presenter at the First Conference on Fee-Based Research in 1982.

SHARON J. ROGERS
University Librarian
George Washington University
Washington, D.C.

Sharon J. Rogers is the University Librarian at George Washington University. Her work at George Washington University has focused on reorganization of the Library from a hierarchial to a collaborative structure, definition of the professional role of librarians as that of a subject specialist, and introduction and elaboration of strategic planning for the library.

From 1978–1983, she served as an information services consultant on a major law case for a Washington, D.C. law firm. In 1978, she consulted with George Washington University on the formation of a fee-based service in Gelman Library, a goal that was finally achieved in 1987 with the inauguration of INQUIRE, which was formed as a response to issues raised in the strategic planning process.

Rogers completed a B.A. in Social Sciences at Bethel College, St. Paul, MN in 1963, an M.A. in Library Science at the University of Minnesota in 1968, and a Ph.D. in Sociology at Washington State University in 1976. She has worked in libraries at Washington State University, The University of Toledo, and Bowling Green State University before arriving at George Washington University in 1984. She also taught sociology at Alfred University. Rogers has been active in the American Library Association and is past chair of the Association of College and Research Libraries.

DEBRA SCHNEIDER
Outreach Services Coordinator
Health Sciences Library
The Ohio State University

Debra Schneider is currently in charge of the Medical and Health Information Service (MHI) in the Health Sciences Library of The Ohio State University. From 1985–1987 she worked at the University of Michigan Libraries in Cooperative Access Services spending half time in Michigan Information Transfer Source (MITS) and half time helping to create 747-FAST, Michigan's library campus delivery service for faculty. During this time she was a participant in the University of Michigan's Research Library Residency program. Ms. Schneider has an M.A. in Library and Information Studies from the University of Wisconsin, Madison and a B.A. in Speech-Communications from the University of Minnesota.

ALICE SIZER WARNER
Information Guild
Lexington, Massachusetts

Alice Sizer Warner, Information Guild (Box 254, Lexington, MA 02173), teaches about, writes about, and consults on the subject of charging fees for information services. She has taught widely at graduate schools of library and information science as well as for professional continuing education programs. Publications include *Mind Your Own Business: A Guide for the Information Entrepreneur* (Neal-Schuman, 1987); a book on fee-based library services is in progress. She is a graduate of Radcliffe/Harvard and of Simmons GSLIS. Awards include election to *Phi Beta Kappa* and *Beta Phi Mu* and a 1986 Simmons Alumni Achievement Award.

FRANCES WOOD
Associate Director, University-Industry Research Program and
Program Director, Information Services Division
Kurt F. Wendt Library
University of Wisconsin-Madison

Frances Wood is employed by the University of Wisconsin-Madison. She is program director of the Information Services Division, Kurt F. Wendt Library, and an associate director of the University-Industry Research Program. Both ISD and UIR are University outreach programs established in the 60s to serve Wisconsin's business community. Under Ms. Wood's leadership and guidance, ISD has developed a wide range of services and presently serves information needs of business and industry throughout the United States and abroad. As UIR associate director, Ms. Wood works closely with faculty and participates in technology transfer and 'update' workshops and seminars.

Ms. Wood holds a library degree from the University of Wisconsin-Madison. She is active in the Wisconsin Library Association and has held various offices in the Wisconsin Chapter of Special Libraries Association. On a national level, Ms. Wood has participated in workshops and seminars at SLA and has presented papers at U.S. patent and trademark workshops.

Conference
Attendees

Abrams, Faye
Coordinator, IBIS
Univ. of Waterloo Library
Waterloo, Ontario, Canada

Ackerman, Katherine
Katherine Ackerman & Assoc.
Lansing Community College
East Lansing, MI

Baker, Gayle
Engineering Library
University of Alabama
Tuscaloosa, AL

Beaubien, Anne K.
MITS
University of Michigan
Ann Arbor, MI

Bosler, Ann
University Libraries
Arizona State University
Tempe, AZ

Burr, Robert L.
Crosby Library
Gonzaga University
Spokane, WA

Casorso, Tracy
INQUIRE — Gelman Library
George Washington Univ.
Washington, DC

Chatfield, Mary
Baker Library
Harvard Business School
Boston, MA

Clark, Georgia A.
Wayne State University
Detroit, MI

Clemens, Linda S.
Ohio State Univ. Library
Columbus, OH

Crowther, Karmen N.T.
University of Tennessee
Knoxville, TN

Dalrymple, Tamsen
Ohio State Univ. Library
Columbus, OH

Dodge, Michael Ross
J.Y. Joyner Library
East Carolina University
Greenville, NC

Downing, Arthur
NY Acad. of Med. Library
New York, NY

Drake, Miriam
Price Gilbert Mem. Lib.
Georgia Inst. of Tech.
Atlanta, GA

Frye, Irene S.
Polytechnic University
Brooklyn, NY

Grant, Mary
CW Post Campus
Long Island University:
Center for Business Research
Greenvale, NY

Grund, Diane
Moraine Valley Comm. College
Palos Hills, IL

Hale, Kathryn
Texas Med. Center Library
Houston Academy of Medicine
Houston, TX

Harvison, Phyllis
Bus. Sci. & Tech. Department
Houston Public Library
Houston, TX

Heller, James
College of Law
University of Idaho
Moscow, ID

Homan, Michael
The Upjohn Company
Corporate Technical Library
Kalamazoo, MI

Hood, Ken
Sci. & Engineering Library
SUNY at Buffalo
Buffalo, NY

Josephine, Helen
Arizona State University
Tempe, AZ

Kearns, Patricia M.
Christopher Newport College
Newport News, VA

Kizis, Carol A.
Sci. & Engineering Library
SUNY at Buffalo
Buffalo, NY

Law, Gordon
Krannert Library
Purdue University
West Lafayette, IN

Lucas, Jane
Kresge Bus. Ad. Library
The University of Michigan
Ann Arbor, MI

Lunden, Elizabeth
North Harris County College
Library
East Campus
Kingwood, TX

Lyle, Stan
Univ. of Northern Iowa
Cedar Falls, IA

Marram, Michele
Baker Library
Harvard Business School
Boston, MA

Martin, David
University of Iowa
Business Library
Iowa City, IA

Marvin, Stephen
ExeLS
Drexel University
Philadelphia, PA

Mikkelsen, June
Multnomah County Library
Central Library Director
Portland, OR

Moylan, Betsey
Alumni Memorial Library
University of Scranton
Scranton, PA

Pensyl, Mary E.
M.I.T.
C.L.S.S., 14 Sm-48
Cambridge, MA

Perry, Bonita
Eisenhower Library
Johns Hopkins University
Baltimore, MD

Person, Ellen
Dept. of Lib. Science Info.
Lansing Community College
Lansing, MI

Poole, Jay Martin
Univ. of California, Irvine
Irvine, CA

Powell, Wayne B.
Lufkin Engineering Library
Tufts University
Medford, MA

Prendergast, Kathleen
Library-ADM
Northwestern University
Evanston, IL

Rhodes, Kathy
Texas Christian Library
Fort Worth, TX

Robison, Carolyn L.
Georgia State University
Atlanta, GA

Rogers, Sharon
Melvin Gelman Library
George Washington University
Washington, DC

Rubens, Donna
University of Minnesota
Minneapolis, MN

Schatz, Natalie
Edwin Ginn Library
Tufts University
Medford, MA

Schloman, Barbara
Kent State University
Kent, OH

Schneider, Deb
Health Sciences Library
Ohio State University
Columbus, OH

Smith, Janet
Industrial Technology Inst.
Ann Arbor, MI

Sutton, Lynn Sorenson
Harper Hospital Library
Detroit, MI

Tomajko, Kathy
Research Info. Services
Georgia Tech. Library
Atlanta, GA

Vaughan, Jim
John Crerar Library
University of Chicago
Chicago, IL

Warmann, Carolyn
Carol Newman Library
VPI&SU
Blacksburg, VA

Warner, Alice Sizer
The Information Guild
Lexington, MA

Weiss, Carla M.
NYS School of Ind. & Lab. Rels.
Cornell University
Ithaca, NY

Wood, Fran
Information Services Division
University-Industry Res. Program
Kurt F. Wendt Engineering Lib.
Madison, WI

Wylie, Nethery
University of Colorado Library
Colorado Springs, CO

Selected Bibliography on Fee-Based Services in Academic Libraries

Debra R. Schneider
The University of Michigan

The focus of this bibliography is on publications which discuss fee-based research in academic libraries. Citations on related topics such as information brokering, marketing, copyright, fee/free issues, administration, and ethical considerations were added selectively.

Aspnes, G. INFORM: an evaluation study on an information service. *Minnesota Libraries* 24, 171–185, Autumn 1974.

Baker, S.K. Fee-based services in the M.I.T. Libraries. *Science and Technology Libraries* 5(2), 15–21, Winter 1984.

Beaubien, A.K. Fees or free: the philosophy behind charging for reference service. In *Reference Service: A Perspective,* ed. Sul H. Lee. Ann Arbor, MI: Pierian Press, 1983, 99–112.

Beaubien, A.K. Michigan Information Transfer Source: fee-based information service. *Library Hi-Tech* 1(2), 69–71, Fall 1983.

Beeler, R.L. and Lueck, A.L. Pricing of online services for nonprimary clientele. *Journal of Academic Librarianship* 10, 69–72, May 1984.

Bellardo, T. and Waldhart, T.J. Marketing products and services in academic libraries. *Libri* 27, 181–194, September 1977.

Bellomy, F.L. The information brokerage scene in America. In *First International On-Line Information Meeting, Proceedings,* London. Oxford: Learned Information, 1978.

Berry, J.N. Breaking down open doors? (research on library fees and marketing) *Library Journal* 108, 526, March 15, 1983.

Birks, C.I. *Information Services in the Market Place.* London: British Library, 1978. (British Library research and development reports, 5430 0308–2385.)

Blake, F.M. and Perlmutter, E.L. Libraries in the marketplace: information emporium or people's university? *Library Journal* 99, 108–111, January 15, 1974.

Borbely, J. Increasing productivity in information services. *Online* 9, 114–117, January 1985.

Boss, R.W. Library as an information broker. *College and Research Libraries* 40, 136–140, March 1979.

Boss, R.W. and Maranjian, L. *Fee-based Information Services: a Study of a Growing Industry.* New York: Bowker, 1980. (Information management series, 1.)

Broadbent, C. Pricing information products and services. *Drexel Library Quarterly* 17, 99–107, Spring 1981.

Buhman, Lesley. Fees-for-information: legal, social and economic implications. *Journal of Library Administration* 4(2), 1–10, Summer 1983.

Burwell, H.P., ed. *Directory of Fee Based Information Services* Houston, TX: Burwell Enterprises, 1985.

Cady, Susan A. and Richards, Berry G. The one-thousand-dollar alternative: how one university structures a fee-based information service for local industry. *American Libraries* 14(3), 175–176, March 1982.

Carter, Nancy C. and Pagel, Scott B. Fees for service: the Golden Gate University Law Library Membership Plan. *Law Library Journal* 77(2), 243–274, 1984–1985.

Casper, C.A. Pricing policy for library services. *ASIS Journal* 30, 304–309, September 1979.

Citron, Helen R. and Dodd, James B. Cost allocation and cost recovery considerations in a special academic library: Georgia Institute of Technology. *Science and Technology Libraries* 5(2), 1–14, Winter 1984.

Conference on Fee Based Research in College & University Libraries, Proceedings. June 17–18, 1982. Center for Business Research: Greenvale, NY, 1982.

Cooper, M.D. Charging users for library service. *Information Processing and Management* 14, 419–427, 1978.

Cooper, M.D. Economics or information. In *Annual Review of Information Science and Technology* ed. Carlos A. Cuadra, vol. 8, 5–40, Washington, DC: ASIS, 1973.

Cronin, B. Public good and private interest, a delicate balance. *Leads* 26, 6–7, Spring 1984.

Cuadra, C. The role of the private sector in the development and improvement of library and information services. *Library Quarterly* 50, 94–111, January 1980.

DeGennaro, R. Libraries, technology, and the information marketplace. *Library Journal* 107, 1045–1054, June 1, 1982.

DeGennaro, R. Pay libraries and user charges. *Library Journal* 100, 363–367, February 15, 1975.

Dodd, J.B. Information Brokers. *Special Libraries* 67, 243–250, May 1976.

Dodd, J.B. Pay as you go plan for satellite industrial libraries using academic facilities. *Special Libraries* 65, 66–72, February 1974.

Donnellan, Anne M. and Rasmussen, Lise. Fee-based services in academic libraries: preliminary results of a survey. *Drexel Library Quarterly* 19(4), 68–79, Fall 1983.

Dougherty, R.M. Fees and subsidies. *Journal of Academic Librarianship* 5, 123, July 1979.

Dougherty, R.M. Fees or subsidies: a revisionist view. *Journal of Academic Librarianship* 7, 323, January 1981.

Dragon, A.C. Marketing the library. *Wilson Library Bulletin* 53, 498–502, March 1979.

Drake, M.A. The economics of library innovation. *Library Trends* 28(1), 89–105, Summer 1979.

Drake, M.A. Information and corporate cultures. *Special Libraries* 75(4), 263–269, October 1984.

Drake, M.A. Managing innovation in academic libraries. *College and Research Libraries* 40(6), 503–510, November 1979.

Drake, M.A. User fees: aid or obstacle to access? *Wilson Library Bulletin* 58(9), 632–635, May 1984.

Edinger, J.A. Marketing library services: strategy for survival. *College and Research Libraries* 41, 328–332, July 1980.

Evans, John. A Feasibility Study for the Development of Fee-Based Services in Academic Libraries: Report to the Vice President for Business and Finance, Memphis State University. May 1984. ERIC document ED260714.

Everett, J.H. *The Information Broker's Handbook: How to Profit from the Information Age.* Lewisville, TX: Ferret Press, 1984.

Ferguson, P. Chronicles of an information company. *On-line Review* 1, 39–42, March 1977.

Finnigan, G. Nontraditional information service. *Special Libraries* 67, 102–103, February, 1976.

Freeman, James E. and Katz, Ruth M. Information marketing. *Annual Review of Information Science and Technology* 13, 37–59, 1978.

Gaffner, H.B. The demand for information-on-demand. *Bulletin of the American Society for Information Science* 2, 10, February 1976.

Garvin, A.P. and Bermont, H. *How to Win With Information or Lose Without It.* Washington, DC: Bermont Books, 1980.

Gilmen, N.J. Library services for health professionals. *California Librarian* 33, 110–113, April 1972.

Heller, J.S. Copyright and fee-based copying services. *College and Research Libraries* 47, 28–37, January 1986.

Heller, J.S. and Wiant, S.K. *Copyright Handbook* Littleton, CO: Published for the American Association of Law Libraries by F.B. Rothman, 1984. (AALL publications series no. 23.)

Hershfield, A. Information counselors: a new profession? *Humanization of Knowledge in the Social Sciences,* ed. Pauline Atherton. Syracuse, NY: School of Library Science, 1972.

Hicklin, K. Reference update: fee-based information services. *Show-Me Libraries* 33, 29–30, June 1982.

Hornbeck, Julia W. An academic library's experience with fee-based services. *Drexel Library Quarterly* 19(4), 23–36, Fall 1983.

Houk, J. Freelancing: keeping it ethical. *Wilson Library Bulletin* 57, 854–855, June 1983.

Howie, E. *Marketing of Information Services.* Diss., University of Pittsburgh, 1977.

Information Broker/FreeLance Librarian, New Careers, New Library Services Workshops, Proceedings,. ed. Barbara B. Minor. Syracuse, NY: Syracuse University School of Information Studies, 1976. (Miscellaneous studies, 3.)

Jensen, R. et al. Costs and benefits to industry of online literature searches. *Special Libraries* 71, 291–299, July 1980.

Journal of Fee-based Information Services January/February 1979 + .

Kaplan, G.M. *Information brokering: A State-of-the-Art Report.* Eugene, OR: Emerald Valley Pub., 1980. (The Business of Information, 1.)

Kasner Morgan, Lynn. Fee-based services in health sciences libraries. *Science and Technology Libraries* 5(2), 23–31, Winter 1984.

Keren, C. and Schwuchow, W. Economic aspects of information services: a report on a symposium. *Journal of Information Science* 3, November 1981.

King, D.W. Pricing policies in academic libraries. *Library Trends* 28, 47–62, Summer 1979.

Kingman, Nancy M. and Vantine, Carol. Commentary on the special librarian/fee-based service interface. *Special Libraries* 68, 320–322, September 1977.

Klement, S. Marketing library-related expertise. *Canadian Library Journal* 34, 97–101, April 1977.

Kok, J. Now that I'm in charge, what do I do? *Special Libraries* 71, 523–528, December 1980.

Kotler, P. *Marketing for Nonprofit Organizations.* Englewood Cliffs, NJ: Prentice-Hall, 1975.

Kotler, P. Strategies for introducing marketing into nonprofit organizations. *Journal of Marketing* 43, 37–44, January 1979.

Kotler, P. and Connor, R.A. Marketing professional services. *Journal of Marketing* 41, 71–76, January 1977.

Lehman, L.J. and Wood, M.S. Effect of fees on an information service for physicians. *Medical Library Association Bulletin* 66, 58–61, January 1978.

Lewis, D.W. Bringing the market to libraries. *Journal of Academic Librarianship* 10, 73–76, May 1984.

Lewis, H.G. *How to Handle Your Own Public Relations.* Chicago: Nelson-Hall, 1976.

Line, M.B. Information services in a technological university: plans and prospects. *Information Scientist* 5, 77–88, June 1971.

Lowrey, P.E. Useful books on information brokerage. *Library Trends* 32, 357–358, Winter 1984.

Lunden, E. Library as a business: conference on fee-based research in academic libraries finds cost recovery mandatory in serving off campus users. *American Libraries* 13, 471–472, July 1982.

Mancuso, J.R. *How to Start, Finance, and Manage Your Own Small Business.* Englewood Cliffs, NJ: Prentice-Hall, 1984.

Maranjan, L. and Boss, R.W. *Fee-Based Information Services: A Study of a Growing Industry.* New York: Bowker, 1980.

McDonald, E. University/industry partnership: premonitions for academic libraries. *Journal of Academic Librarianship* 11, 82–87, May 1985.

McLaughlin, B.E., comp. *Marketing of Professional Services: A Bibliography.* Syracuse, NY: Information Services and Research, 1979.

Mintz, A.P. Information practice and malpractice: do we need malpractice insurance? *Online* 8, 20–26, July 1984.

Mintz, Anne P. Information practice and malpractice. *Library Journal* 110(15), 38–43, September 1985.

Monson, G. Coping with the demand. *American Libraries* 6, 72, February 1975.

Mount, Ellis, ed. Fee-based services in sci-tech libraries. *Science and Technology Libraries* 5(2), 1–50, Winter 1984.

Mowat, I.R.M. Who pays for what? (services offered by a university library) *SLA News* 183, 3–5, September/October 1984.

Newlin, B. 200 questions: how Information on Demand contracted with the North Suburban Library System. *Library Journal* 107, 151–153, January 15, 1982.

Nicholson, N.N. Service to industry and research parks by college and university libraries. *Library Trends* 14, 262–272, January 1966.

Nort, J.H. and Wheeler, M.W. Library service by contract: a joint venture. *College and Research Libraries* 28, 107–109, March 1967.

Parker, J.S., ed. *Information Consultants in Action.* London, New York: Mansell Pub., 1986. (Information adviser series.)

Penland, P.R. *Information Consultants and Learning Brokers* Pittsburgh: University of Pittsburgh, 1979.

Penner, R.J. The practice of charging users for information services: a state-of-the-art report. *Journal of the American Society for Information Science* 21(1), 67–74, January/February 1970.

Pooler, J. and Weber, D.C. Technical information services in the Stanford University Libraries. *College and Research Libraries* 25, 393–399, September 1964.

Popovich, C.J., ed. Fee-based information services in academic and public libraries. *Drexel Library Quarterly,* Fall 1983.

Raffin, M., ed. *The Marketing of Information Services: Proceedings of a Seminar Held by the Aslib Information Industry Group,* May 11, 1977. London: Aslib, 1978.

Reid, Richard C. Fee-based services and collection development in an academic library. *Drexel Library Quarterly* 19(4), 54–67, Fall 1983.

Richards, Berry B. and Widdicombe, Richard P. Fee-based information services to industry. In *International Association of Technological University Libraries Meeting* (11th: 1985: Oxford, Eng.). *The Future of Information Resources for Science and Technology and the Role of Libraries.*

Rochell, Carlton. The knowledge business: economic issues of access to bibliographic information. *College & Research Libraries* 46(1), 5–12, January 1985.

Rowley, A.M. Local information services for business and industry in the East Midlands. *Journal of Librarianship* 4, 70–73, January 1972.

Saldinger, J. Full service document delivery: our likely future. *Wilson Library Bulletin* 58, 639–642, May 1984.

Shapiro, B.P. Marketing for nonprofit organizations. *Harvard Business Review,* 51, 123–132, September/October 1973.

Shapiro, S.J. Marketing and the information professional: odd couple or meaningful relationship. *Special Libraries* 71, 469–474, November 1980.

Schick, P. Information for sale. *Library Association of Alberta Bulletin* 6, 148–156, July 1976.

Schwarz, S. Information services to industry: the role of the technological university library. *Journal of Documentation* 32, 1–16, March 1976.

Schwuchow, W. Fundamental aspects of the financing of information centers. *Information Storage and Retrieval* 9, 569–575, October 1973.

Service to business: the fee question. *Library Journal* 100, 1182, June 15, 1975.

Smith, J.I. Marketing information products. In *Humanization of Knowledge in the Social Sciences,* ed. Pauline Atherton. Syracuse, NY: School of Library Science, 1972.

Smith, J.S. Conflict of values: charges in the publicly funded library. *Journal of Librarianship* 13, 1–8, January 1981.

Spencer, L.D. Growing demand for information-to-order. *Savvy* 2, 20–23, January 1981.

Spyers-Duran, P. and Mann, T. W. *Financing information services; problems, changing approaches, and new opportunities for academic and research libraries.* Westport, CT: Greenwood Press, 1985 (New directions in librarianship, 6.)

Tertell, Susan M. Fee-based services to business: implementation in a public library. *Drexel Library Quarterly* 19(4), 37–53, Fall 1983.

Thorelli, H.B. and Engledow, J.L. Information seekers and information systems: A policy perspective. *Journal of Marketing* 44, 9–27, Spring 1980.

Trudell, L. Communicating in the online industry: how an information broker uses electronic mail. *Online* 7, 60–64, November 1983.

Ungarelli, Donald L. and Grant, Mary M. A fee-based model: administrative considerations in an academic library. *Drexel Library Quarterly* 19(4), 4–12, Fall 1983.

Venett, A.J. Technology transfer for industry and business through the university library. *Special Libraries* 72, 44–50, January 1981.

Vormelker, R.L. Industrial research and the academic library. *Journal of Education for Librarianship* 9, 60–71, Summer 1968.

Waldhart, T.J. and Bellardo, T. User fees in publicly funded libraries. *Advances in Librarianship* 9, 36–37, 1979.

Walker, M. *Advertising and Promoting the Professional Practice.* New York: Hawthorn, 1979.

Warner, A.S. Bridging the information flow: a view from the private sector. *Library Journal* 104, 1791–1794, September 15, 1979.

Warner, A.S. Information services—new use for an old product. *Wilson Library Bulletin* 49, 440–444, February 1975.

Warner, A.S. Selling consulting services, buying consulting services. In *Managing the Electronic Library,* ed. Michael Koenig. New York: Special Libraries Association, 1983. (Library management, 3.)

Warnken, Kelly. *The Information Brokers: How to Start and Operate Your Own Fee-Based Service* New York: Bowker, 1981 (Information management series, 2).

Warnken, K. and Felicetti, B., eds. *So You Want to be an Information Broker?* Chicago: Information Alternative, 1982.

White, M.S. Information for industry—the role of the information broker. *ASLIB Proceedings* 32, 82–86, February 1980.

White, M.S. Information trader. *Library Review* 27, 206–208, Winter 1978.

White. M.S. *Profit from Information: How to Manage an Information Consultancy.* London: Andre Deutsch, 1981.

Wilkin, A. Some comments on the information broker and the technological gatekeeper. *ASLIB Proceedings* 26, 477–482, December 1974.

Wood, F.K. KNOW (Knowledge Network of Wisconsin) and ISD (Information Services Division). Special Libraries Association, Contributed Papers Sessions, 66th Annual Conference, Chicago, June 8–12, 1975.

Wood, M.S., ed. *Cost Analysis, Cost Recovery, Marketing and Fee-Based Services: A Guide for the Health Sciences Librarian.* New York: Haworth Press, 1985.

Zurkowski, P.G. Cost effective information. *Library Journal* 100, 1045, June 1, 1975.